UNIPA Springer Series

Editor-in-Chief

Eleonora Riva Sanseverino🆔, Department of Engineering, University of Palermo, Palermo, Italy

Series Editors

Carlo Amenta🆔, Department of Economics, Management and Statistics, University of Palermo, Palermo, Italy

Marco Carapezza, Department of Human Sciences, University of Palermo, Palermo, Italy

Marcello Chiodi, Department of Economics, Management and Statistics, University of Palermo, Palermo, Italy

Andrea Laghi, Department of Surgical and Medical Sciences and Translational Medicine, Sapienza University of Rome, Rome, Italy

Bruno Maresca, Department of Pharmaceutical Sciences, University of Salerno, Fisciano, Italy

Giorgio Domenico Maria Micale, Department of Industrial and Digital Innovation, University of Palermo, Palermo, Italy

Arabella Mocciaro Li Destri, Department of Economics, Management and Statistics, University of Palermo, Palermo, Italy

Andreas Öchsner, Esslingen University of Applied Sciences, Southport, QLD, Australia

Mariacristina Piva, Department of Economic and Social Sciences, Catholic University of the Sacred Heart, Piacenza, Italy

Antonio Russo, Department of Surgical, Oncological and Oral Sciences, University of Palermo, Palermo, Italy

Norbert M. Seel, Department of Education, University of Freiburg, Freiburg im Breisgau, Germany

The **UNIPA Springer Series** publishes single and co-authored thematic collected volumes, monographs, handbooks and advanced textbooks on specific issues of particular relevance in six core scientific areas. The issues may be interdisciplinary or within one specific area of interest. Manuscripts are invited for publication in the following fields of study:

1- Clinical Medicine;
2- Biomedical and Life Sciences;
3- Engineering and Physical Sciences;
4- Mathematics, Statistics and Computer Science;
5- Business, Economics and Law;
6- Human, Behavioral and Social Sciences.

Manuscripts submitted to the series are peer reviewed for scientific rigor followed by the usual Springer standards of editing, production, marketing and distribution. The series will allow authors to showcase their research within the context of a dynamic multidisciplinary platform. The series is open to academics from the University of Palermo but also from other universities around the world. Both scientific and teaching contributions are welcome in this series. The editorial products are addressed to researchers and students and will be published in the English language.

The volumes of the series are single-blind peer-reviewed.

Book proposals can be submitted to the *UNIPA Springer Series Technical Secretariat* at unipaspringer@unipa.it
At the following link, you can find some specific information about the submission procedure to the Editorial Board: https://www.unipa.it/strutture/springer/

More information about this series at https://link.springer.com/bookseries/13175

Elisabetta Di Stefano · Carsten Friberg ·
Max Ryynänen
Editors

Aesthetic Perspectives on Culture, Politics, and Landscape

Appearances of the Political

Editors
Elisabetta Di Stefano
Department of Humanities
University of Palermo
Palermo, Italy

Carsten Friberg
Copenhagen, Denmark

Max Ryynänen
School of Arts, Design and Architecture
Aalto University
Espoo, Finland

ISSN 2366-7516　　　　　　　ISSN 2366-7524　(electronic)
UNIPA Springer Series
ISBN 978-3-030-77829-3　　　ISBN 978-3-030-77830-9　(eBook)
https://doi.org/10.1007/978-3-030-77830-9

© The Editor(s) (if applicable) and The Author(s), under exclusive license to Springer Nature Switzerland AG 2022
This work is subject to copyright. All rights are solely and exclusively licensed by the Publisher, whether the whole or part of the material is concerned, specifically the rights of translation, reprinting, reuse of illustrations, recitation, broadcasting, reproduction on microfilms or in any other physical way, and transmission or information storage and retrieval, electronic adaptation, computer software, or by similar or dissimilar methodology now known or hereafter developed.
The use of general descriptive names, registered names, trademarks, service marks, etc. in this publication does not imply, even in the absence of a specific statement, that such names are exempt from the relevant protective laws and regulations and therefore free for general use.
The publisher, the authors and the editors are safe to assume that the advice and information in this book are believed to be true and accurate at the date of publication. Neither the publisher nor the authors or the editors give a warranty, expressed or implied, with respect to the material contained herein or for any errors or omissions that may have been made. The publisher remains neutral with regard to jurisdictional claims in published maps and institutional affiliations.

This Springer imprint is published by the registered company Springer Nature Switzerland AG
The registered company address is: Gewerbestrasse 11, 6330 Cham, Switzerland

Preface

Appearances of the Political (Ap.pol.) is the name of a network that was initiated as a so-called study-circle in the Nordic Summer University (NSU), and that, after 3 years of Nordic Funding, continued as an autonomous group of academics, students, and independent scholars. Within the framework of NSU, six seminars were held, beginning in 2016 in Riga (Latvia) and proceeding to Orivesi (Finland), in 2017 in Wrocław (Poland) and Saulkrasti (Latvia), to conclude the presence in NSU in 2018 in Copenhagen (Denmark) and Fårö (Sweden). Raine Vasquez, Laine Kristberga, and Noora-Helena Korpelainen were among the coordinators of these seminars. Later seminars were held in Marina di Ascea (Italy) in 2018, and in Espoo (Finland) and Cēsis (Latvia) in 2019. An international cooperation agreement was signed during a one-day conference at the University of Palermo to formalise future projects in 2018.

This book is not the simple outcome of those meetings, but a work of some participating scholars along with invited authors to broaden the horizon of the investigation. A publication of some presentations from the NSU-seminars have already been published in a thematic issue of *Popular Inquiry: The Journal of the Aesthetics of Kitsch, Camp and Mass Culture* (Vol 1, 2019; eds. Noora-Helena Korpelainen, Olivia Glasser, and Emily Aiava), intitled *Appearances of the Political. Anthology*.

The working code of the Ap.pol.-network is democratic and interdisciplinary, which calls forth challenges. Cross and interdisciplinarity are popular on research agendas; however, there is often the naïve belief that the mere fact of bringing methods and disciplines together makes it interdisciplinary. We believe that it is important to find common ground for research while also recognising our diversity. Both "appearances" and "political" are large fields that require a line of characteristics. The various contributions in this anthology are approaches to the theme rather than attempts at definitions. Any definition in itself is an appearance of ideas enabling a view of something and could be construed as a political act of taking control over discourses and directing them towards specific intentions.

We would like to thank the University of Latvia, the University of Wrocław, the University of Copenhagen, Wassard Elea, the University of Palermo and Aalto University for hosting our international meetings, and also thank others for funding (Palermo, Aalto) our activities.

Over 100 people have been involved. Besides the authors of this book and the ones already mentioned, we would like to pick some and express our gratitude to allies, supporters, and participators—thank you Pauls Daija, Johanne Aarup Hansen, Eret Talviste, Corinna Casi, Minna Heikinaho, Henrik Juel, Gioia Laura Iannilli, Bill Thompson, Epp Annus, Iiris Konttinen, Giedre Vaicekauskiene, Rosita Vaičiule, Neli Dobreva, Monika Favara-Kurkowski, Anete Vanaga, Lars Aagaard-Mogensen, Liliana Coutinho, Arnold Berleant, Sune Frølund, and Mira Kallio-Tavin—and all those who just joined for an hour or a day for discussion, or signed their names, somewhere, on a paper that made everything possible.

Palermo, Italy	Elisabetta Di Stefano
Copenhagen, Denmark	Carsten Friberg
Espoo, Finland	Max Ryynänen

Introduction

Some titles are mysterious and attractive, others direct and clear; in any case, each title aims to entice people to read the book. However, we learn not to judge the book by its first appearance: the cover or the title.

This book is about "appearances". It aims at investigating the "appearances of the political" through analysis and characterisations that contribute to explain the dimension of contemporary cultural phenomena. This wide field has been focused on through eight different approaches, but first it is useful to give a brief explanation to our common understanding of "appearances" and "the political" and secondly a motivation for taking an interest in this topic.

An apperance is a semblance, what we sense which is an aspect of something, a phenomenon, or an occurrence. The appearance of a person makes us care for the appearance itself, i.e. what is immediately present to us such as the bodily posture, the dress, and forms of communication that affect us, and also for who we believe to be behind the immediate presence. It is in a similar way we ask ourselves about the appearances of the political. Appearances are not only what is made present to us but also about what is written between the lines or hidden under the surface. Something can be right in front of us, but we pay no attention to it because we are blinded or we are too occupied elsewhere.

The reader will notice that a common point of reference in the book is aesthetics. So why do we speak about appearances rather than aesthetics? A short answer could be for strategic reasons. A problem about aesthetics is that in a lot of traditions, it has a too narrow significance for what is intended here. It is often limited to art and beauty, while we want to include several other fields and discussions. We wish to include researchers and practitioners that do not think of their work in relation to aesthetics but nevertheless work in the same field as we wish to address.

In recent decades, we have witnessed more nuances to the concept of aesthetics. In the 1980s and 90s, aestheticisation began to widen the field of aesthetics to cultural phenomena in general—something already present in cultural critiques but then usually with a critical view rather than descriptive. Later, Everyday Aesthetics became established as an independent research focus to discuss how to apply the concept of aesthetics outside the dominant limitation to art and beauty. Since the

1910s, the artworld has itself struggled with the institutional imprisonment of art and sought to break the boundaries in different ways often to politicise ordinary events or to make us aware of the implicit political components appearing perhaps in anonymous cultural disguise. Since the year 2000, we can find research into atmosphere/ambiance. This is a multi-sensorial field of studies of the environment that unites both aesthetics and appearances using sensorial as a keyword; this field includes material culture studies, human geography, sociology, urban studies, and anthropology, just to name some.

Since the mid-twentieth century, cultural and political critiques have debated different perspectives of culture and its political dimensions, and we have recently found an increasing number of such studies in relation to, for example, gender and race as well as the material and biological environment. Obviously, the discrimination of specific groups of people embedded in behaviour, seen as fundamental cultural norms, is an example of an appearance of the political; so it is the planning of an infrastructure for the benefit of particular interests and discrediting others—and likewise the design of everyday objects and institutions—that embody behaviour and habits.

This brings us to a comment on the use of the adjective used as a noun: "the political". In this book, we do not refer to politics merely understood as explicit decision processes and as strategies of governing, but we aim to highlight in what way political forms appear in different fields (culture, education, environment). The examples above show us how, in the 1970s and '80s, one could come across the statement that everything is political. To say "everything is political" does not mean anything. We must differentiate as to what can be seen as political and in what way, and of course we also need to be more precise as to what political includes. Without settling for a specific understanding of the political, we can say it relates to power, to forming, influencing and organising opinions, decisions and actions both explicit, and to be found implicit in cultural phenomena.

The political goes beyond a direct intervention to influence or organise social environment. We should not limit our focus to explicit political agendas. However, we may find our social interactions influenced and shaped by settings that must be characterised as political. We are deeply influenced by political ideals and structures that we do not pay attention to. Living in a Western, democratic society, we will find ideals of democratic culture influencing how we organise things, making us expect a degree of transparency in organisations, the possibility of questioning decisions and decision processes, perhaps a form of participation whether directly or through representatives. Likewise, less visible political elements form our every day. Western living is based on an economic order which implies elements of inequality between members within the society and globally. Any product we buy is the end result of a long chain of production and distribution that only exists because we actively, but more often passively, agree to the elements of power and decisions upholding these chains. They exceed by far what we know and are aware of; even the conscious consumer will struggle with getting sufficient information to make a choice in accordance with ideals. The complexity and inaccessibility of receiving information are often an excuse for not acting—we could never learn, comprehend, or act on the information about every consumer choice we make. However, the choice of not acting is a choice of consent to a political order, even if we are not fully aware of what order it is.

The societies we live in and our language are even more complex. If we agree that, in line with Aristotle, human being is a *zōon logon ekhon*, a "living being capable of speech"; we understand that we speak because we belong to a community—we speak to others. We organise our lives in relation to a community, taking into account our idea of ourselves and people, and we exchange our understanding of this organisation with others.

According to Aristotle also, some animals live in communities but they do not reflect on and discuss ideals of societal order. We experience that the community organises our life before we can even reflect upon it. We also find that the language we speak forms a relation to our environment, a relation which makes something present to us while simultaneously creating a distance to the world. While speaking we can get a hold of things, but how and what to hold can be disputed, and holding something—to have something in one's hand—is a matter of power. In language, we find a permanent negotiation about the world. Today, we can witness this in discussions about terms and notions to use, and especially not to use, because they both denote something and connote a relation to that something.

Language is never neutral, the words we use can be excitable and performative. While speaking there can be something written between the lines, often something we are not in control of ourselves, yet we convey messages through this "something". I may be made aware that I am using a language, others hear as a language of a group with a social position. When faced with it, I realise that what I thought was neutral is not neutral and what I thought to utter with a sentence becomes also a statement of political content. In addition, I often have no choice. Take an example of the use of prepositions. When I speak about the large island in the North Atlantic, do I say "on Greenland" or "in Greenland"? "On" an island or "in" an autonomous territory? Do I recognise the political status of its people or do I maintain a colonial position? And I have no choice of not using a preposition!

A reference to Aristotle is likewise, no neutral reference to an ancient Greek philosopher; it is a reference to a figure of immense importance for the Western scientific language dominating within a current political order of global dominance. The point here is not to make research relative and limit its truth value to only the culture it appears in. It is important to keep in mind that despite cultural and political differences, we do communicate; we would never have any disagreements and conflicts if we did not have a common ground to argue from.

Finally, taking up this theme of appearances of the political should be given a motivation.

The statement, from the 1970s and '80s, that everything is political disappeared in the postmodern discourses that became an academic trend during the '80s. At first, it appeared as though the postmodern had abandoned the political focus. Their critics, often from the previous generation, would complain that the postmodern meant giving away the political sense and critical approach to instead thoughtlessly embracing new cultural forms. The postmodern would, on the other hand, insist the old generation was blind to transformations due to new media, new global outlooks, new economic experiments, and the collapse of old ideological and political systems. The postmodern did not as such abandon a political focus but what they abandoned was largely the narratives of the old ideologies. Some twenty-first century critics have complained that postmodern cultural analyses have ended in fragmentation and relativity and consequently lose their political potential. They become only singular agendas without a view of fundamental political structures. If there is a postmodern legacy, it may be a distaste for narratives holding a utopian ideal of the grand finale at the cost of concrete phenomena such as ecology and environmental issues, and questions of social and human relations like human rights, gender, and identity—the latter a theme that appears in many forms from sexual to national. Lately, global issues such as climate and inequality bring back discussions regarding political and economic systems asking for rethinking them without the pathos of giving ultimate answers.

Hence, it seems that the political has been transformed into new forms. To talk of a return of the political in academic contexts is probably too much. We should rather say that in some contexts the political returns, or perhaps it was there all along but it appeared in different ways. We should probably also say that some new approaches focus on particular issues but are uncomfortable with the larger narratives of recent past which recede from pursuing topics to the end. There is perhaps still the need to being reminded about the "everything is political", or if not everything, at least to pay more attention to how the political appears. We should, perhaps, acknowledge that the political may be present in both what we have not considered as such and in what we do take as political discourses, but it appears in a form different from that expected. As the grand narratives may become blind to details, the singular analyses may lose the larger perspective.

An objective for academic analyses of the political may be to how single-targeted political discourses of today—like climate change that at the turn of the decade into the 2020s has rocketed to the top of political agendas in many countries—are far deeper embedded in political elements than what we believe when we discuss concrete and "visible" issues such as how to reduce emissions. It may turn out to be a discussion about a specific lifestyle. While it appears easy to argue about the material standards of modern conveniences from running water, fridges, and healthy houses to acquiring means of transportation, communication, and entertainment, it is not always easy to see whether they are "means" for convenient living or the "goal" of existence. It is less easy to see if these are only material standards. Consumerism is no political ideology, but it may be a political force transforming many places to conform to ideals of society and politics based on specific forms of economy and what is considered their necessary layout.

One may take a moment to reflect on what we plug into with our electronic devices. Is, for example, the phone a tool to help us solve practical problems? Or is it a device invading our lives, offering services that create dependencies and habits formed by certain (commercial) interests? In recent years, it has proved to be an essential tool for political activism. It has also proved to be a tool of surveillance, of the same activists as well as consumers. These tools prove to be complex and contradictory, when on the one hand they are used by activists facing inequality and oppression, and on the other they are a means for the exact same inequalities being integrated into the system of consume and market that exploits economically and socially weak citizens elsewhere. We are using such means and products even though we may be aware that they are problematic. Nevertheless, we show little intention of changing our habits—we may even choose to turn a blind eye on the problems.

Such questions have motivated the forming of the network *Appearances of the Political*. Many current political analyses, discourses, and actions are directed towards explicit issues like abusive and violent behaviour, industrial food production, and the discrimination of particular groups of people. However, this network is motivated by bringing awareness to what in our everyday life does not attract much attention, and also to the analysis which has still not been given much consideration.

We acknowledge the wide variety of related work done in various fields of humanities and social sciences, although we feel that our own reflection has taken a different route. There are already classical works written by Theodor W. Adorno, Herbert Marcuse, Leo Lowenthal, Max Horkheimer, Walter Benjamin, and Henri Lefebvre. We have learned a lot from the distinguished contemporary humanities-driven approaches of Crispin Sartwell's *Political Aesthetics* (Ithaca: Cornell University Press, 2010), Jacques Rancière's *The Politics of Aesthetics* (London: Bloomsbury, 2013), Arnold Berleant's *Sensibility and Sense: The Aesthetic Transformation of the Human World* (Exceter: Imprint Academic, 2010), and Gernot Böhme's *Critique of Aesthetic capitalism* (Milan: Mimesis International, 2017). We also acknowledge how much these issues pop up in art theory (Sezgin Boynik & Minna Henriksson eds., *Contemporary Art and Nationalism: Critical Reader,* Pristina: Institute of Contemporary Art "EXIT", Center for Humanistic Studies "Gani Bobi", 2007), in design (Albena Yaneva. *Five Ways to Make Architecture Political. An Introduction to the Politics of Design Practice.* London: Bloomsbury 2017), and in research on social science, for example: Judith Halberstam (*In a Queer Time and Place: Transgender Bodies, Subcultural Lives,* New York: New York University Press, 2005), John Street ("Aesthetics, policy and the politics of popular culture", in *European Journal of Cultural Studies*, Vol. 3, 2000, Issue 1:27–43), Eeva Luhtakallio ("Group formation, styles, and grammars of commonality in local activism", in *British Journal of Sociology,* 2018) and Ana Sofia Elias, Rosalind Gill et al. (*Aesthetic Labour: Rethinking Beauty Politics in Neoliberalism (Dynamics of Virtual Work),* New York: Palgrave MacMillan, 2018). This issue is present in studies of cultural forms and their expressions like in Sara Ahmed (*The Promise of Happiness.* Durham: Duke University Press 2010), and points out how new technologies alter our fundamental perception of political culture (Shoshana Zuboff. *The Age of Surveillance Capitalism. The Fight for a Human Future at the New Frontier of Power.* London: Profile Books 2019). Obviously, it is a thematic of the crossing of cultural critique and activism; to give only one example, we can mention The Nanopolitics Group (Paolo Plotegher, Manuela Zechner and Bue Rübner Hansen, *Nanopolitics Handbook,* Wivenhoe: Minor Compositions, 2013). They are approaches that seem to come to the same territory, just from different sides of the theoretical landscape. With our book, we hope to recollect some thinking that lies at the intersection of disciplines, and to bridge at least some of this lack of interdisciplinary dialogue.

This anthology is a step in this process, or eight different steps to approach a common interest. Mandoki's (*Aesthetic Politics and Political Aesthetics: A Crucial Distinction*) and Ryynänen's (*Political Concepts as Aesthetic Concepts*) papers focus on some concepts useful to highlight the notion of political aesthetics. The first points out the differences between "political aesthetics", understood as the aesthetisation of politics to optimise the impact of propaganda, and "aesthetic politics", as the use of politics to impose a regime of a particular aesthetic ideal, underlining their contrasting and decisive social outcome. The second highlights the way aesthetics colours political concepts to the extent that sometimes when we think we are discussing politics, we are discussing only its aesthetics.

The following two essays focus on the issue of formation. Elisabetta Di Stefano (*Care as Key to Political Aesthetics*) investigates the concept of care starting from the ancient idea of care, from Socrates and Plato to Italian Humanism, as a way of educating ourselves and others to live a good life. She understands care as a tool for political aesthetics, seen as a theory of sensitiveness in the relational space of a city. Carsten Friberg claims in *The Body in Formation. Reflections on Body Bildung* that the formation of the body is essential also for the formation of the spirit. We are often left with the impression that the Western philosophical tradition is unwilling to recognise the role of the body. This is the impression we get from many standard readings we encounter. However, it gives us a false and biased understanding of the Western thinking and education and it is furthremore potentially dehumanising.

The successive two papers focus on the concept of democracy from different perspectives. Tonino Griffero (*Staged Emotions. Is a Democratic Atmospherization a Contradictio in Adjecto?*) reflects upon the fact that, while imagining atmospheres in politics, we normally think of the aestheticisation of politics put in place by an authoritarian and totalitarian regime and not of democracy. Based on a neophenomenological approach to aesthetics, the atmospheric potential (also) of democracy is sketched for discussing a "provisional atmospheric morality". In *Neutral Arts to Democratic Values. The Case of Iranian Naghashi-Khat (Calligram)*, Majid Heidary points out how some arts may promote social and democratic values while others promote non-democratic tenets, and he focuses on a case study: *Naghshi-khat* (Iranian Calligram) as a good example of neutral arts to democracy. Being formal, abstract, and decorative, this artistic genre replaces the seemingly valid picture of the governments' ideology with the lived experience of people through national symbolism and poetic appearance.

Finally, the last two paper essays focus on landscape that is a central issue in politic agendas. Mateusz Salwa shows in *Landscape Aesthetics and Politics* that the landscape conceived as an aesthetic phenomenon has a conspicuous political significance. Understanding aesthetics in line with the original meaning of the term (i.e. as denoting sensory experience), landscapes turn out to be aesthetic insofar as they are sensory environments. As such, they are political at their core, as any such environment is shaped by politics. Hence, landscapes may be defined as sensory appearances of the political. It, then, seems advisable that landscape aesthetics should play a conspicuous role in landscape theory dominated by sociological, economic, and cultural approaches. Moving within a larger framework of environmental and ecological aesthetics, Margus Vihalem *(The Beauty of Nature at Risk of Extinction! Could Aesthetics act as Means for Saving Natural Beauty?)* asks whether perceiving the nature of beauty could serve to have a more responsible attitude towards nature. According to him, aesthetics—based on the awareness and respect for natural beauty—can make us change our attitude and initiate a long-awaited trasformation in the general political perception of the environment.

These eight approaches show us different appearances of the political and remind us that political ideas appear in different forms, and a given form reveals political implications: the medium itself is a form of appearance of the political.

Contents

Aesthetic Politics and Political Aesthetics: A Crucial Distinction 1
Katya Mandoki

Political Concepts as Aesthetic Concepts 17
Max Ryynänen

Care as Key to Political Aesthetics 27
Elisabetta Di Stefano

The Body in Formation. Reflections on Body Bildung 41
Carsten Friberg

Staged Emotions. Is a Democratic Atmospherization a Contradictio in Adjecto? 59
Tonino Griffero

Neutral Arts to Democratic Values. The Case of Iranian Naghashi-Khat (Calligram) 71
Majid Heidary

Landscape Aesthetics and Politics 83
Mateusz Salwa

The Beauty of Nature at Risk of Extinction! Could Aesthetics Act as a Means for Saving Natural Beauty? 101
Margus Vihalem

Editors and Contributors

About the Editors

Elisabetta Di Stefano is graduate cum laude both in Classical Literature and Philosophy (Ph.D. in Aesthetics and theory of Arts). She is Associate Professor at the University of Palermo, where she teaches Aesthetics both in the Department of Humanities and in the Department of Architecture. She is a member of the "Italian Society of Aesthetics" (SIE) and the "Société internationale Leon Battista Alberti" (SILBA). Moreover, she is in the board of a new international journal: *Popular Inquiry: The Journal of the Aesthetics of Kitsch, Camp and Mass Culture*. Her research focuses on three fields: the theory of the arts in the Renaissance; the ornament theory; the aesthetics of everyday life with particular reference to architecture and design. Currently, she is part of a research group that is developing everyday aesthetics in Italy. She has published in a variety of international journals (Aesthetica Preprint; Rivista di Estetica, Aisthesis) and she has participated in many international conferences. Main publications: *L'altro sapere. Bello, Arte, Immagine in Leon Battista Alberti*, Palermo, Centro Internazionale Studi di Estetica, 2000; *Estetiche dell'ornamento*, Milano, Mimesis, 2006; "The Aesthetic of Louis H. Sullivan: Between Ornament and Functionality", in *Ornament Today*, ed. Joerg Gleiter, (Bozen: University Press, 2012), 64–75; *Iperestetica. Arte, natura, vita quotidiana e nuove tecnologie,* Palermo, Centro Internazionale Studi di Estetica, 2012; *Everyday Objects*, eds. Giovanni Matteucci, Elisabetta Di Stefano, Andrea Mecacci, *Aisthesis*, n. 1 (2014); *Che cos'è l'estetica quotidiana*, (Roma: Carocci, 2017); *Designing Atmospheres. The Role of Aesthetics in the Requalification of Space*, in Mario Bisson (a cura di), *Environmental Design. 2nd International Conference on Environmental Design,* DE LETTERA WP, Milano, 2017, pp. 15–21; *Cosmetic Practices: The Intersection with Aesthetics and Medicine* in *Aesthetic Experience and Somaesthetics,* ed. by Richard Shusterman, Series: Studies in Somaesthetics, Leiden-Boston, BRILL, 2018, pp. 162–179; *Art in the street. Artification Strategies for Public Space*, in "3rd International Conference on Environmental Design", ed. Mario Bisson, (3–4 October 2019, Marsala, Italy), Palermo University

Press, 2019, pp. 121–126; *From Familiar to Uncanny. Aesthetics of Atmospheres in Domestic Spaces*, "Proceedings of the 21st International Congress of Aesthetics, Possible Worlds of Contemporary Aesthetics: Aesthetics Between History, Geography and Media" (ICA2019), 22–26 July 2019, Belgrad, Serbia, University of Belgrade—Faculty of Architecture, pp. 1750–1756; *The Power of the Gift. A Perspective of Political Aesthetics*, in "Popular Inquiry. The Journal of the Aesthetics of Kitsch, Camp and Mass Culture", vol. 1, 2019, special issue "Appearances of the Political Anthology", Noora-Helena Korpelainen, Olivia Glasser, and Emily Aiava (Eds.), pp. 26–35 (https://www.popularinquiry.com/).

Carsten Friberg is cand.phil. (MA) & Ph.D. (2004) in philosophy from the universities of Odense and Copenhagen, Denmark. He has held positions as assistant and associate professor at Aalborg University (2012–14); assistant professor at Aarhus School of Architecture (2007–11); assistant professor and external lecture at Copenhagen University (1995–2000 and 2003–7). He is currently working as freelance researcher and teacher, including teaching at University of Southern Denmark and Kolding School of Design. He is appointed external examiner by the Ministry of Research for Philosophy, The Creative Educations (design and architecture) and Performance Design (2018–22), and has previously been appointed to Design Studies (2014–18). He was head of the board of Nordic Summer University (2013–14) where he has coordinated more study circles (2007–10 and 2015–17). Scientific key words are aesthetics, atmosphere/ambiance, aesthetic education, philosophy of culture, political philosophy, theory of science/artistic research, phenomenology, hermeneutics, and philosophical anthropology. His work is often placed in a cross-disciplinary context including working with practitioners. He has published *Æstetiske erfaringer* (*Aesthetic experiences* 2007) and edited anthologies: w/Ulrik Bisgaard *Det æstetiskes aktualitet* (*The actuality of the aesthetic* 2006), w/ Esther Oluffa Pedersen & Per Jepsen *Kants kritik af dømmekraften—otte læsninger* (*Kant's critique of judgement—eight readings* 2007), w/Rose Parekh-Gaihede & Bruce Barton *At the Intersection Between Art and Research. Practiced-Based Research in the Performing Arts* 2010, w/Raine Vasquez *Experiencing the Everyday* 2017. He has published peer-reviewed articles in *Studi di estetica, Popular Inquiry,* Ambiances. International Journal of Sensory Environment, Architecture and Urban Space, *Nordicum Mediterraneum, Nordic Journal of Architectural Research, Artifact, The Nordic Journal of Aesthetics* and 20 proceedings/book chapters, most recent »The Aesthetic Endeavour in an Age of *Halbbildung:* Some Questions about Taste«, in Aagaard-Mogensen & Forsey, eds. *On Taste: Aesthetic Exchanges.* Newcastle, Cambridge Scholars Publishing, 2019, 41–52. He has given more than 50 conference presentations in 20 different countries and been peer reviewer for journals, among more, *Artifact*; *Emotion, Space and Society*; *Journal of Aesthetics and Phenomenology*; *Nordic Journal of Architectural Research*; *Studies in Art and Architecture*; *Gastronomica*; *Media International Australia*; *Journal of Problem Based Learning in Higher Education*; *Journal of Somaesthetics*; *Ambiances Journal*; and for conferences like 2nd International Congress on Ambiances; 8th International Conference on Tangible, Embedded and Embodied Interaction; EKSIG Conference 2015 and 2017; Cumulus 2017 and 2018.

Max Ryynänen is a Helsinki-based scholar in aesthetics, art theory, and cultural studies. He studied in Helsinki University, Uppsala University, Pisa University, and Temple University Philadelphia, and defended his Ph.D. in Helsinki University 2009. He was the chair of the Finnish Association for Aesthetics 2014–2018 and a member of the board of the International Association for Aesthetics 2013–2018. Currently, Ryynänen is the Editor-in-Chief of two journals, *The Journal of Somaesthetics* (together with Falk Heinrich and Richard Shusterman) and *Popular Inquiry: The Journal of the Aesthetics of Kitsch, Camp and Mass Culture* (together with Jozef Kovalcik). He works as Senior Lecturer of Theory of Visual Culture (tenured) at Aalto University in the greater Helsinki region since 2006. Ryynänen is the editor of many books, e.g. *Art and Excess* (Palgrave 2019), with Kevin Tavin and Mira Kallio-Tavin, *Aesthetics in Dialogue* (forthcoming, Peter Lang 2020) with Zoltan Somhegyi, and *Aesthetics of Popular Culture* (Slovart 2014) with Jozef Kovalcik. He has published in a variety of journals, including *Poetics, Contemporary Aesthetics, Terra Aestheticae, Nordic Journal of Aesthetics, The Journal of Comparative Literature and Aesthetics, The Journal of Somaesthetics*—and art journals like *Flash Art International, Art Pulse, Kunstkritikk, Framer* and *Atlantica Internacional*. His special focus is on popular culture, the art scene, and issues of visual culture. His latest publication are *Learning from Decay: Essays on Architectural Deleriction and its Concumption* (Peter Lang 2018, with Zoltan Somhegyi) and "From Haunted Ruin to the Most Touristified of All Cities" in Jeanette Bicknell, Jennifer Judkins and Carolyn Korsmeyer (Eds.), *Philosophical Perspectives on Ruins, Monuments and Memorials* (Routledge, 2019).

Contributors

Elisabetta Di Stefano Palermo, Italy

Carsten Friberg Copenhagen, Denmark

Tonino Griffero Rome, Italy

Majid Heidary Mashhad, Iran

Katya Mandoki Prado Coapa, Mexico

Max Ryynänen Helsinki, Finland

Mateusz Salwa Warszawa, Poland

Margus Vihalem Tallinn, Estonia

Aesthetic Politics and Political Aesthetics: A Crucial Distinction

Katya Mandoki

Abstract Much has been written on the relation between aesthetics and politics since Walter Benjamin's reflections on the aesthetization of politics. In fact, aesthetics has constituted an immensely powerful resource for political use throughout different historical periods in legitimizing regimes, denouncing injustice and persuading or intimidating the population. Yet few have noted that aesthetics and politics connect with each other through two radically different types of articulation: aesthetic politics and political aesthetics, an asymmetric correlation with various social implications. This paper analyses such asymmetry and argues for the necessity to distinguish political aesthetics as the aesthetization of politics to optimize propaganda's impact, from aesthetic politics as the use of politics to impose a regime of a particular aesthetic ideal. We will examine both articulations, often treated indistinguishably, and highlight their contrasting and decisive social outcomes.

Keywords Aesthetic politics · Aesthetic regimes · Benjamin · Fascism · Foucault · Nazism · Political aesthetics · Political artist · Propaganda · Sensibility

Introduction: The Construction of Political Imaginaries

Aesthetics, generally understood as the philosophical study of art and beauty, has been considered a positive value almost by definition as if it would magically endow legitimization to whatever is associated with it. However, there are many other aesthetic categories besides beauty and many uses and abuses of the aesthetic beyond art, most saliently as an instrument for a political agenda by propaganda and as a mechanism for producing power effects. This determinant aspect has intrigued me since my Ph.D. dissertation on Aesthetics and Power (1991) until today. What I did not realize then is that there is yet another articulation between the political and the aesthetic where these terms are inverted. I am referring to aesthetic politics in the strict sense, where the political is the instrument for an aesthetic agenda. At first sight, this combination

K. Mandoki (✉)
Jerusalem, Israel
e-mail: kmandoki@gmail.com

appears worthy and valuable, nearly indistinguishable from political aesthetics but after a close examination, its deleterious implications become manifest.

We must begin by the question of what does politics—as the discussion, negotiation and execution of social power—have to do with aesthetics as the theory of sensibility including art, beauty, and its many other categories and practices. Why do these two diametrically different aspects of social reality appear so insistently linked? One answer is that no political system can be preserved indefinitely by brute force. It requires a degree of acquiescence by the masses. Antonio Gramsci's concept of "hegemony" proposes that organic intellectuals operate as ideological persuaders for the dominant classes to obtain such assent (Luciano 1972). How hegemony is attained to legitimize a Nation–State is a question of constructing and propagating some narratives and imaginaries rather than others for appealing to and being introjected by the population. Althusser (1977: 75–138) contributed to this discussion by defining the role of ideological State apparati and their mechanism of "interpelation" by which each person recognizes her/himself as a subject of and subject by the dominant ideology. However, he never elucidated further how such interpelation is produced or how each person responds to it and manages to identify with the proposed ideology, nor did Gramsci sufficiently explain how these organic intellectuals succeed to persuade the masses. Here the relevance of aesthetics to politics becomes salient.

Anderson (2000: 6) defined a nation as an "imagined political community—and imagined as inherently limited and sovereign." He stated that "communities must be distinguished, not by their falsity/genuineness, but by the style in which they are imagined" (note here the term "style" to which we will return later). This emphasis on the imaginary comes from the fact that members of national communities cannot really know or meet each other, but still imagine themselves as part of a community defined as "nation". The components of such imaginaries are, as I have argued elsewhere, aesthetic (Mandoki 2007b, 2015). National imaginaries and their narratives, like religious, economic, historical or political imaginaries and narratives by which groups cohere, concur, communicate and build their identities must have a strong aesthetic appeal and a dramatic vein to be effective.

Politics and Aesthetic Visibilization

Hannah Arendt (1958: 198) points out that: "The polis, properly speaking, is not the city–state in its physical location; it is the organization of people, since it arises from acting and speaking together, and its true space is found among people who live together for this purpose, no matter where they are." Politics is what happens between people through various activities, real and imaginary, besides the Habermasian communicative action and rational argument (that are too abstract for generating a sense of national cohesion and collective identification).

The majorities of the indigents bearing the economic burden of privileged minorities in regimes of notorious social imbalance could overturn their oppressors simply by their sheer number. To counteract this possibility, strategies are deployed to impose stability on the system and maintain the illusion that a contingent situation is natural, necessary and inevitable. Among the procedures and tactics to achieve this effect of inevitability of the status quo—let's call it a fatalistic fallacy that would presuppose that if a situation exists is because it should exist and persist—we can count the disciplinary technologies widely analyzed by Michel Foucault (1979, 1983). This keen observer of power mechanisms describes a particularly effective and imposing strategy where the subject by power is subjected to and by processes of visibilization. Foucault's analyses on regimes of visibility, however, are not sufficiently explicit about the unavoidable role of aesthetics in the manifestation of power and how it operates to demand it, enforce it, or resist it. I believe such omission is due to Foucault's restricted concept of "aesthetics of existence" derived from the Greeks denoting an ethical life as a work of art and dietetics regulating one's pleasure. Yet he comes across several instances in Surveiller et punir where aesthetic strategies are explicit: (a) The dramatic spectacle of torture and public execution of the regicidal Robert-François Damiens as a *mise-en scène* of the king's power and (b) the eminently aesthetic panopticon effect, not as an artwork or beautiful architecture but in its subjective impact of penetration and conformation of prisoners' sensibility as if being constantly patrolled from the vigilance tower (similar to religion's introjected sin-patrolling god).

Through aesthetics power messages manage to affect the subjects' sensibility and resolutely impact their decision-making (where resistance, docility or admiration, disgust, attraction, compliance are at stake). Thus a prominent mechanism by which political systems address their subjects is and has been aesthetic in the struggle for political hegemony, legitimization, and idealization of its own class image not only by means of art (as Eagleton 1990 contends in the case of the bourgeoisie) but by all aesthetic resources for heightening and intensifying experience as well as numbing it.

This link between power and aesthetic visibilization has been so intimate and compelling that the material traces we inherited from the most stratified societies since antiquity to the present attest to the deliberate ostentation of power by aesthetic means through pyramids, temples, palaces, ceremonial sites, reliefs, mausoleums and cathedrals to contemporary stadiums, shopping malls, financial centers, casinos, mega-hotels, airports, museums, and skyscrapers.

With the development of media and digital technology, as well as with contemporary diffusion and massification of communication, the opportunity to affect and stamp the minds of the population with elaborate imagery for political control has increased exponentially. The invention of photography with its effect of reality and its potential for image alteration, and cinematography with its tremendous emotional impact through narratives, editing, amplification and propagation, as well as its integration of multiple perceptual and aesthetic registers all easily manipulate the real and the imaginary by the ability to create credible fictions and conceal undesirable realities.

Political visibilization is displayed not only via the visual but by the exact same four registers (acoustic, somatic, lexic or verbal and visual or scopic) by which artistic aesthetics are displayed (music, opera, dance and theater, as well as literature, poetry and plastic arts) (cf. Mandoki 2007a, b). These four registers operate in the aesthetic construction of national and other collective identities (tribal, religious, professional, athletic) contributing with narratives in the lexic; settings, props and costumes in the scopic; intonation, pauses volume, music, timbre, tone, and rhythm in acoustic and the theatralization of the leaders acting in ceremonies for the visibilization of their power in the somatic register.

Aesthetics–Politics Tension

The aesthetic and the political are two distinct dimensions of human reality (as the economic, technological, cognitive, ethical, semiotic, biological, geographical etc.) that partially interlock, collide or overlap affecting each other. Since Plato's expulsion of some poets, painters and story-tellers from the Republic to Aristotle's Rhetorics involving aesthetics in deliberative political persuasion (as "verbal beauty" by metaphors and other figures of speech or as poets' voice on stage by hypokrisis) to German idealist philosophers like Winckelmann, Herder and Schiller who promoted the "political artist" and the "artistic State", and moreover to Frankfurt School philosophers' view of art for emancipation and ideological conscientization, the pertinence of the relation between aesthetics and the political is only increasing.

Frank R. Ankersmit's Aesthetic Politics (1997) analogy of political representatives and represented with artworks and their subject matter is correctly questioned by Crispin Sartwell (2010: 97) on the grounds that "[t]he relation of representation here does not obtain between "the people" and a person but inheres in the political system qua person itself, in the Hobbesian sense." Furthermore, Arnold Berleant's (2010: 201) demolishing critique on Ankersmit's text points out its false presuppositions and logical flaws, among other problems, given that "arguments from analogy have a weak logical status for they are suggestive rather than demonstrative."

Perhaps the most frequently quoted author on this subject matter is Jacques Rancière (2004: 140) who claims that "If there is such thing as an 'aesthetics of politics', it lies in a re-configuration of the distribution of the common through political processes of subjectivation. Correspondingly, if there is a politics of aesthetics, it lies in the practices and modes of visibility of art that re-configure the fabric of sensory experience." It is problematic that Rancière alternates from a definition of the aesthetic as the perceptual in general on one hand and as theory of art on the other, or as Kant's First Critique's a priori while he defines politics as a form of experience (which actually characterizes aesthetics, not politics). "I mean here 'aesthetic' in a sense close to the Kantian idea of 'a priori forms of sensibility': it is not a matter of art and taste; it is, first of all, a matter of time and space." (2005: 13) But then adds "my work on aesthetics was aimed at re-framing the temporal categories by means of which modern and contemporary artistic practices are generally grasped." Again: "In Disagreement, I tried to conceptualize that 'aestheticity' of politics in general."

(2005: 14) Yet: "The entire question of the 'politics of aesthetics'—in other words, of the aesthetic regime of art..." (2005: 116).

Rancière maintains this ambiguity, as he proposes a wide conception of the aesthetic related to the perceptible, but actually reduces it to the "regime of the arts". Despite the very limited effect art regimes have upon the population's sensorial experience since they are by definition elitist, he contends that "[a]esthetics refers to a specific regime for identifying and reflecting on the arts ... defining the connections within this aesthetic regime of the arts." Here again: "... 'aesthetic practices' as I understand them, that is forms of visibility that disclose artistic practices, the place they occupy, what they 'do' or 'make' from the standpoint of what is common to the community." (2005: 13) In Dissensus (2010: 143) he proposes to discuss "which models of the efficacy of art govern our strategies, hopes and judgments regarding the political import of artistic practice?".

Politics of aesthetics for Rancière imply a dispute against what he calls the police's "distribution (partage) of the sensible". However, it rather seems that it is we, the ordinary people, who create political space among ourselves in all directions: (bottom up, sideways, obliquely, top bottom, center and periphery) as the macroscale protest in Hong Kong taking the streets and the screens by visibilizing their number through bodies, lights, helmets, umbrellas, smartphones and other aesthetic props to protest against economic and juridical issues. Moreover, politics are expressed not only in speaking and imaging but in physically positioning and sonorizing through a variety of dramaturgical verbal and non verbal acts (marches, rituals, gestures of domination or subordination, distances or proximities, passivity or activism etc.) as well as by continuous and quotidian micro-physical non dichotomic (people-State) operations of power along the whole social spectrum to negotiate, impose or resist conditions which undeniably have effects on perception and forms of experience.

This problematic and relevant relation of the political and the aesthetic is taken also by Crispin Sartwell (2010: 1–2, 238) holding that: "Not all art is political, but all politics is aesthetic; at their heart political ideologies, systems, and constitutions are aesthetic systems, multimedia artistic environments." He clarifies: "I've characterized political aesthetics as being concerned with the aesthetic features of political systems, not the political features of aesthetic systems" (Sartwell 2010: 99). We definitely concur in this distinction, yet it becomes disorienting when, on the other hand, he claims that: "[P]olitical ideologies and constitutions are aesthetic systems of which texts form a portion, in the precise sense that political systems appear in different media, none of which is fundamental and all of which are related; the ideology or system in part simply is the design style" (2010: 2).

I have repeatedly argued that the aesthetic dimension has relevance throughout all social institutions or matrixes, not only the State, as other cultural dimensions have, among them the political, the economic, ethical, semiotic, educational, environmental, biological, technological dimensions. (cf. Mandoki 1991, 1992, 2007a, b ch. 28–32) Every institution produces its own particular conventions of style and design, but this does not turn the political into "aesthetic systems" or into Rancière's "art regimes" even if they can always be observed through an aesthetic lens, since there are other applicable lenses as there are dimensions.

A politics is an aesthetic environment, whatever else it may be. Political systems are no more centrally textual than they are centrally systems of imagery, architecture, music, styles of embodiment and movement, clothing and fibers, furnishings, graphic arts. It's not that systems use these things as tools to gain loyalty, for propaganda; it's that a military junta, sharia law, and anarchism, for example, constitute artpolitical environments in all media (Sartwell 2010: 2).

This statement is problematic on various instances. First the claim that politics are an aesthetic environment confuses the specificity of the political with its aesthetic effects, and the aesthetic with its political effects as well as the State with all political and aesthetic activity. As I argue above, politics are operated through arendtian "acting and speaking together" in all social institutions by what Foucault defined as "micro-physics of power", not only by the State. There are politics in the family, in a classroom, in a church, a scientific community or a hospital, as there are aesthetic, economic and semiotic practices in them.

Second, why does Sartwell think that such imagery, architecture, music turn politics into specific artpolitical systems rather than being just part of the perceptible, sensorial fabric of social reality, and consequently can be found, again, in all institutions, not only the State and not only through political activity? Politics, like aesthetics, ethics, semiotics, allow me to insist, is a social dimension that can be traced throughout all cultural matrixes (i.e. religious, medical, family, judicial, artistic, the State, sports or educational as I have discussed in other texts Mandoki 1991, 1992, 1994, 2007a, 2007b).

Third, the notion of "artpolitical environments" is not sufficiently defined, seemingly due perhaps to a presupposed identity between art and aesthetics that slips also through Rancière's texts. However, aesthetics, as the theory of sensibility (originally founded as such by Baumgarten's scientia cognitionis sensitivae) examines one distinct dimension of social and biological life among the various other regions, dimensions and patterns that constitute reality: the sensitive dimension. Art, on the other hand, is a specific institutional convention upon particular sets of objects and events, as Dickie (1974) accurately argued, that are placed as candidates for aesthetic (I would say "artistic") appreciation (as other objects are candidates for economic consumption by aesthetically enticing marketing).

From an objectualistic and formalistic approach to aesthetics Sartwell (2010: 5) asserts: "It seems to me that a rough idea of aesthetic properties as properties of a thing's design or configuration (conceived as an arrangement of materials) under an interpretation will suffice." Yet things only "have" designs or configurations in terms of perceptual subjects' semio-sensorial processes within particular conditions of interpretation (semiotic, biological, social, cultural). It is a matter of sensibilities involved, and not of inherent formal qualities of the objects themselves or a supposed autonomous thingness.

Fourth, I wonder why Sartwell considers military juntas or sharia law as "artpolitical environments". What is artistic about them? It is true that a regime's imposition of enclosing a woman's head within a burqa or hijab seriously constricts her sensorial universe (which would best illustrate Rancière's police distribution of the sensible) with unequivocally negative aesthetic effects, but the question is whether these two cases are still political or rather its nullification given that they do not allow any social negotiation "among people living together" but inflict despotic enforcement upon their female population. People who fight for political principles fight for very concrete present and future conditions of life and well-being for their children and neighbors, not for artpolitical environments, as the global women's protest against violence and feminicide attest (cf. BBC link on women's 2019 protests below).

Political Aesthetics and Its Strategies: Five Cases

Political aesthetics radically differ from aesthetic politics yet, as we have seen, their meaning seems to be shifting in theoretical works dealing with this connection. Since a pragmatics approach requires unequivocal definitions to keep the meaning stable and apt for analysis, we consequently demarcate a clear distinction between political aesthetics on one hand referring to politics that utilize aesthetics as a persuading tool towards its own ends and on the other hand aesthetic politics which denote the politicization of aesthetics or aesthetics operating politically to accomplish a particular aesthetic ideal.

To illustrate this fundamental and contrasting articulation of the political and the aesthetic in each specific direction, we will briefly examine five cases of political aesthetics or the deliberate use of the aesthetic for political purposes. Four cases have in common that they are produced from official political agents: the Unknown Soldier ritual in the United Kingdom, Obama's 2008 presidential campaign, China's 70th revolution anniversary parade in 2019 and Mexico's 2018 presidential inauguration ceremony. The fifth is unofficial and anti-official overflowing into an international gender protest: women's performance "A rapist in your path". The four cases are targeted toward citizens top to bottom, even if their style could not be more diverse, whereas the women's performance is targeted to all, sideways and bottom top, but specifically pointing to the State as well as to male citizens.

Case 1

Anderson brings up the classic example of nationalism expressed through the Unknown Soldier memorial. The cenotaph is an aesthetic construction designed to produce the emotional effect of admiration towards individuals who sacrificed their life for the homeland. The brutality of war forces the State to transmute such horror into honor by displaying aesthetic strategies that glorify all these too many violent and premature deaths. Thus, at the end of the First World War, King George V established in 1918 the Memorial Day ceremony in honor of the fallen soldiers to be commemorated every 11 of 11 at 11 in Commonwealth countries. This ceremony shifts from the dominant scopic of the Milite Ignoto Altare in Rome to the dominant somatic of political figures' presence at that time and place to awaken patriotic emotions performed at the cenotaph (cenotaph means in Greek empty tomb). Formations of soldiers, religious choirs, ecclesiastical figures, and military bands march, pray and sing while offerings of crowns of red poppies are placed at the monument.

During the 2005 London ceremony, 20 veterans used lights to send a message from the roof of the Royal Observatory on the Thames River to the parade of the mounted guard that would be decoded at Whitehall. The message said "War turns us into stone. In memory we shine and rise to new days." Two Douglas Dakota DC3 aircraft scattered three million poppy petals over London and the bridges of the Thames. The London Eye 2 lit up red during the commemoration. To the right of the bishop, Queen Elizabeth displayed in tone and form the gestures indicated for the ceremony wearing a black suit and hat. Days before, the members of the Royal British Legion carried a paper poppy on the lapel, symbolizing the blood shed by soldiers on the battle front since 1918, a symbol inspired by John McCrae's 1915 poem In Flanders fields. Evidently all this choreography, props and settings, recitations and songs do not bring back to life the prematurely dead soldiers nor make them known. It is all an aesthetic display for legitimizing the State and the military.

Case 2

Established regimes use onerous resources to aesthetically exhibit their power and create the sense of their indispensability. People's Republic of China celebrated its 70th Anniversary with a colossal, scrupulous and massive human machine-like military parade by 100,000 performers and soldiers with a precision and discipline never seen before, particularly impressive in the Chinese female soldiers' performance. This seems to have been the biggest most meticulous aesthetic demonstration of power since the Zeppelin Field formation designed by Albert Speer. By its sheer heftiness and effacement of individuality and of the human within the vast incalculable quasi robotic deployment in synchronicity and sacrifice of the personal for the collective, such aesthetics of order and control provoke fear of being crushed by the homogenization of this social machine and at the same time relief of being dispensed from individuality and merge into this invulnerable giga-mass. To such enormous somatic display we must add the acoustics of 70 cannon rounds and concert gala The Nation Moves Onward, plus the spectacular scopic props of 70 Dongfeng-41, 160 flying aircraft, 600 tanks and other weapons paraded through Chang'an avenue, the same of the unforgettable image in which a single man tried to stop a row of tanks with his body in June 4, 1989 (one of the most poignant images ever). (cf. Mandoki 2008).

Case 3

Candidates that aspire to captivate voters during electoral campaigns deploy primarily aesthetic strategies that present the candidate according to carefully designed identity models calculated by marketing engineers and image consultants to seduce or fascinate their potential voters, exactly as identities are designed to commodities for commercial marketing campaigns to fascinate their potential consumers. Not by coincidence the same professionals are hired in both cases. Candidates are displayed as detergents, cars, sport shoes, beverages or star system celebrities since they are also a kind of commodity. They obey to the same aesthetics and logic of mass culture consumption developed by Madison Avenue's advertising agencies using the same persuasive mechanisms such as repetition, hyperbolization, simulated personalised interpelation, product panegyrics targeting each social niche by aiming at their particular sentimental kitsch.

During the American 2008 presidential elections, Black Eyed Peas group singer Will.I.am created a hip hop video clip that turned out to be a very improved version of the 1985 celebrities self-complacent kitsch We are the world. He made a collage of a fragment of the Democratic candidate's speech that would evoke Martin Luther King's speech "I have a dream", with the acoustic seduction of rhythm and hip hop recruiting the symbolic weight of the racial struggle to capitalize over a mulatto candidate as an Afro–American (who in fact is exactly as much white as he is black).

The video made use of 37 attractive celebrities (musicians, actors and athletes) that during 4'30" repeat as a choir the campaign slogan Yes we can. They were carefully selected as tokens to represent particular fractions of the North American society, namely African–Americans, Asians, Latinos, Jews, gays, single mothers, disabled and Puerto-ricans, a variety in reality fictitious because these celebrities are of the same type: mostly 30–40 years old, sexy, hot, super-cool, good-looking and successful. The repetitive slogan "yes we can" is pronounced as a quasi-prayer with religious reverberations, adding the visuals of beautiful faces in very well elaborated black and white format to create an effect of sobriety and naturalness. This video to support a presidential candidate proved to be a masterpiece of political propaganda, the American contemporary equivalent to Riefenstahl's Triumph of the Will. Using hip hop aesthetics to recruit Afro–American voters and transfer the fans' esteem for their stars to the candidate through the bandwagon effect by the well-known advertising tactics that exploit status bias, all proved very effective in achieving viral contagion, since in American society such models are mainly entertainment and sports celebrities. The now ex-president owes his electoral success in a large extent to the aesthetics of this video clip that reached more than 26 million viewers (not much compared to Eminem—Love The Way You Lie ft. Rihanna 1,863,946,063 but significant for a political clip), which was followed by another Will.I.am's creation with messianic and personality cult tints whose motto is "Obama" (among other artists who promoted him).

Case 4

Aesthetic strategies for political use can also be quite grotesque. By sharp contrast to professional advertisement image construction of a candidate and of the British and Chinese discipline and control, an improvised aesthetic show was concocted for the inauguration ceremony of the new president of Mexico, Andrés Manuel López Obrador, who in December 1, 2018 used and abused autochthonous Indian tokens to make himself appear as if magically anointed with a supposedly symbolic cane and a crucified Jesus cross as a leader of Mexico's native ethnic and Catholic populations (blatantly violating the Leyes de Reforma's radical separation of Church and State, a 19th century achievement). These token indigenous performers were later reprimanded by their community leaders for playing this role and violating their own traditions. This fake Mexican-curious new-age kitsch performance full of incense, ribbons, smoke and magic, ominously foreshadowed the improvised political style, anti-scientific rhetoric, opaque disbursements, moralistic prudishness and lack of organization that characterize López's regime since.

Case 5

Politics in the arendtian "acting and speaking together…" have an eloquent recent example in women performing "A rapist in your path" around the world during the first half of December 2019. Public plazas were taken to protest aesthetically by rhythm, lyrics, dancing and performing against violence upon women and machism's blaming the victims. A group of Chilean performers, Lastesis, composed a danced-rhymed protest in the chorus "El violador eres tú" against the high rate of feminicide and rape (about 10 women killed daily in Mexico) a protest replicated in many cities from Chile to Turkey and India. The main signifier is body language, rhythm and the number of women united in unison and unicorporeity choreographically projecting empowerment to contrast the traditional victimized, submissive female image. Across youtube, one can trace this sudden spontaneous anti-official aesthetic manifestation, also directed against the carabineros and police who prominently figure among the rapists. By the aesthetics of dance and lyrics not for the sake of beauty but of safety, strength and justice these women call for a universal gender solidarity and awareness.

In short, the aesthetics of politics are deployed through an immense variety of aesthetic strategies and throughout various registers, scales, directions, styles, and categories from the most sophisticated and intimidating to the cool, energetic, disciplined, and the desperate, vulgar, ridiculous, courageous, fake and even the coarse (v.g "The Center for Political Beauty" recently used human ashes taken from Nazi extermination camps for an "art" installation in Berlin, definitely a very odd idea of "beauty").

Aesthetic Politics and Its Sinister Core

While the aesthetics of politics as analyzed previously is a deliberate display of emotional and sensibility-arousing mechanisms for political purposes, the politicization of aesthetics or the politics of aesthetics attempts to impose a particular idea of beauty or its own version of the aesthetic by a political deployment. The aestheticization of politics is manipulative whereas the politicization of aesthetics is impositive and ultimately ensues into different forms of fascism, totalitarianism and despotism inflicting upon the population an arbitrary idea of beauty stemming from personality cult or an idolization of racial, military, war and violence standards.

The historical trend that ultimately gave rise to the politicization of aesthetics is delineated in Josef Chytry's (1989) *The Aesthetic State*, according to whom the first German to dream an imaginary Aesthetic State inspired by the Greeks was Winckelmann, followed by von Herder, Goethe, Hegel and Schiller. In the Letters on the Aesthetic Education of Man, Schiller proposed the "political artist" who is endowed with the power to design humans as his material for an utopian aesthetic State: "… the state is an organisation which fashions itself through itself and for itself, and for this reason it can only be realised when the parts have been accorded to the idea of the whole" (Schiller 1795: IV, c.f. Mandoki 2019: 2). Mussolini (1922) declares "the task of Fascism is to make the mass an organic whole with the Nation, […] just as the artist takes his raw material in order to create his masterpiece." Thus the Statesman as artist has the perfect alibi for every form of violence, all for the sake of a particular idea of beauty.

Nazism's relation to aesthetics deployed not only the aestheticization of politics through propaganda by Riefenstahl, Speer, and Goebbels but mainly the politicization of aesthetics. On one hand Joseph Goebbels, Minister of the Reich of Public Instruction and Propaganda who completely controlled the theater, literature, press, radio, film and art, is the paradigmatic example of aesthetics used by totalitarian regimes to manipulate the masses (cf. Mandoki 2003). Aesthetics here are a means for a political end as depicted in the previous section of this text. *Mein Kampf* is splattered not only with these aesthetics of politics (such as the redesign of the swastika, common in Austrian antisemitic far-right circles) but mainly with the politics of an aesthetics obsessed with a particular image of racial beauty. "The supreme purpose of the ethnic State is to guard and preserve those racial elements which, through their work in the cultural field, create that beauty and dignity which are characteristic of a higher mankind."

On Nazi aesthetic politics Susan Sontag (1975) notes the following: "It was in the SS that this assertion seemed most complete, because they acted it out in a singularly brutal and efficient manner; and because they dramatized it by linking themselves to certain aesthetic standards. The SS was designed as an elite military community that would be not only supremely violent but also supremely beautiful." Or both, violence became beauty.

Sartwell (2010: 12, 16, 18) credits Hitler in Mein Kampf "for making full identification of the political and the aesthetic" and proposes that "Nazism as an aesthetic is described as a synthesis of romanticism and classicism, a sublimization of the classical." He adds: "One way to formulate the effect of a Nazi romantic classicism is that it articulates German national culture—its language, its arts, and its "Aryan" bodies—as the particular repository of universal values, an aesthetics of German world conquest." Moreover: "… Hitler dealt with the bureaucratic structure, or with military planning, or with genocide, from the point of view of an aesthetic sensibility and for the sake of an aesthetic effect…" leaving us uncertain as to how operating genocide is possible from aesthetic sensibility rather than crass insensibility and sheer visceral hatred.

His "Holocaust Aesthetics" section is particularly unfortunate on several accounts: it does not distinguish between artworks that deal with experiences of the Holocaust, (i.e. Adorno's corrected reference to poetry about Auschwitz) and the Holocaust itself as aesthetic phenomenon if this can even be conceivable, namely the torment of sensibility involved in incommensurable suffering at labor and extermination camps. Given that the ordinary use of the term "aesthetics" is equaled to beauty "Holocaust aesthetics" could dangerously be taken to mean "the beauty of genocide", as perverse as "rape aesthetics", "torture aesthetics", "pedophilia aesthetics" or snuff aesthetics.

In fact, we are not dealing here with a mere matter of style but with a depraved genocidal supremacist organization which not only deployed aesthetic strategies such as mass soldier formation in Speer's light and sound effects (the "cathedral of light" in Zeppelinfeld) choreographic marches and massive gymnastic maneuvers plus the grotesque goose step and zieg heil gesture, in addition to swastika graphics, Wagner's compositions as musical score for Nazi stagings, and the *Uber Alles*, *Horst Wessel Lied*, *Vorwärts, Vorwärts* songs and hymns plus the führer's delirious rhetoric and gesticulations, swastika and monumental banners plus Nazi officers' uniforms designed by Hugo Boss (Mandoki 2003). All these are politics' aesthetic tools with diverse artistic quality from Riefenstahl's mastery to Hitler's kitschery and hysterics. Rather than this aesthetization of politics, what was uniquely sinister here was its politization of aesthetics that, as Frederic Spotts (2009: 10) keenly observed, consisted on the fact that Hitler "regarded politics not art as a means to an end, the end of which was art." When the arbitrariness of art and "beauty" for their own sake alone are the goal by political means, genocide is lurking.

Nazi mystification of the artist is described in what Isaiah Berlin saw in Napoleon; "the sinister artist whose materials are men—the destroyer of old societies and the creator of new ones—no matter at what human cost: the superhuman leader who tortures and destroys in order to build new foundations…." (quoted by Spotts 2009: 11) Hitler saw himself as Staatkünstler, artist of a State. Goebbels said of Hitler, admiringly: "His creativity is that of a genuine artist, no matter in what field he may be working." (Spotts 2009: 43) A genocide artist.

Conclusion

We have examined the double articulation between politics and aesthetics alerting against generalizing views that conflate all politics as aesthetic or all aesthetics as political without regard to the asymmetries involved and their serious social repercussions. I have argued that while the aestheticization of politics attempts to achieve a political agenda utilizing aesthetic means, the politicization of aesthetics is deployed to impose an aesthetic version of the State as a work of art by political means.

Walter Benjamin ([1936] 1968: 241) alerted that the *Ästhetisierung der Politik* characterizes all forms of fascism: "All efforts to render politics aesthetic culminate in one thing: war". Although he uses both articulations interchangeably, he didn't imply only politics' propagandistic use of aesthetics in the shifting meaning of the "aestheticization of politics", but given the context of Nazi agenda through prevalent politicization of aesthetics, it also encompasses the exaltation of war and violence to legitimize the extermination of whatever it decrees goes against its particular aesthetic ideal. As stated by Marinetti:

> For 27 years we Futurists have rebelled against the branding of war as antiaesthetic... Accordingly we state: ... War is beautiful because it establishes man's dominion over the subjugated machinery by means of gas masks, terrifying megaphones, flame throwers, and small tanks. War is beautiful because it initiates the dreamt-of metalization of the human body....
> (Benjamin quoting Marinetti [1936] 1968: 241)

Marinetti is partly right in that all these have a tremendous aesthetic impact upon our sensibility, but wrong as to the category of applied (he falls into the usual conflation of the aesthetic and the beautiful). For its victims and other sensitive perceptors and witnesses, war is everything but beautiful. It is terrorific. Benjamin ([1936] 1968: 242) adds "Its [mankind's] self-alienation has reached such a degree that it can experience its own destruction as an aesthetic pleasure of the first order. This is the situation of politics which Fascism is rendering aesthetic. Communism responds by politicizing art." Communism, an economic model, politicizes art using it for propaganda in socialist-realism, while Fascism, an aesthetic model, deploys politics to impose its aesthetics of war, violence, and race. (cf. Jay 1992) Benjamin was pointing at a different more sinister phenomenon: his prophetic view later evidenced in Karlheinz Stockhausen and Damien Hirst's aesthetic admiration of the 9/11 attack and in many contemporary artists and aestheticians that consider 9/11 and Hiroshima and Nagasaki atomic bombings as "sublime" objects of contemplation disregarding the real sensibility at stake: human agony that can not in any way be categorizable. Here the relevance of understanding the aesthetic strictly in its original etymological sense denoting sensibility—rather than a qualifying honorific title endowed to certain objects—is mandatory.

There is nothing objectionable with aesthetic politics that seek to preserve beautiful landscapes, improve the aesthetic qualities of cities, enhance aesthetic appeal in education, and encourage aesthetic values for the well-being of the population. Taking care of the aesthetic dignifies human life. However, while the political can promote various objectives depending upon the institution in which it is exercised, the function of a State is exclusively administrative for the common good in guaranteeing human rights and enforcing the Law. Thus an "Aesthetic State" not only transgresses its role as guarantor of the security of its citizens but becomes a tool for an individual or a group's particular idiosyncrasy of "beauty" and art that can easily derive into eugenics. The State is not, and should never be, an end in itself nor political in relation to the people it serves, only in relation to other States (in acting and speaking together). Whenever a State invests disproportionately in aesthetic exhibitions of itself, it is a clear index that it is concealing vital issues from the public eye, in particular a degree of violence. The State requires technological, military, scientific, and economic expertise for such complex social tasks since ancient hydraulic and tributary modes of production, and the only legitimate articulation of terms here is not a political aesthetics nor aesthetic politics but ultimately ethical politics, a political deployment for a universally ethical State responsible for the well being of citizens.

A decade earlier, Benjamin expressed the grim omen of imminent catastrophe that would devour also him: "The most rabidly decadent origins of this new theory of war are emblazoned on their foreheads: it is nothing other than an uninhibited translation of the principles of *l'art pour l'art* to war itself." In other words, what was at stake here was a state pursuing the political aesthetics of war.

> ... the one, fearful, last chance to correct the incapacity of peoples to order their relationships to one another in accord with the relationship they posses to nature through their technology. If this corrective effort fails, millions of human bodies will indeed inevitably be chopped to pieces and chewed up by iron and gas ([1936] 1979: 128).

As they were. Can we ever learn?

References

Althusser L (1977) Ideología y aparatos ideológicos de Estado. Posiciones. Grijalbo, México, pp 75–138
Anderson B (2000) Imagined communities. Verso, New York
Ankersmit FR (1997) Aesthetic politics: political philosophy beyond fact and value. Stanford University Press, Stanford
Arendt H (1958) The human condition, 2nd ed. University of Chicago Press, Chicago
Benjamin W (1930) 1979. Theories of German Fascism: on the Collection of Essays War and Warrior edited by Ernst Jünger. New German Critique 17:120–128
Benjamin W (1936) 1968. The work of art in the age of mechanical reproduction. In: Illuminations. Shoken Books, New York, pp 217–25
Berleant A (2010) Sensibility and sense, the aesthetic transformation of the human World. Imprint Academic, Charlottesville
Chytry J (1989) The aesthetic state: a quest in modern German thought. University of California Press, Berkeley and Los Angeles
Dickie G (1974) Art and the aesthetic: an institutional analysis. Cornell University Press, New York
Eagleton T (1990) The ideology of the aesthetic. Blackwell, Oxford
Foucault M (1979) Microfísica del poder. La Piqueta, Madrid
Foucault M (1983) Vigilar y Castigar; nacimiento de la prisión, 8th ed. Siglo Veintiuno, México.

https://www.bbc.com/news/world-50557784f?fbclid=IwAR3E_wdQwRSGtpWbGNmUmO4EIO Aq3hLeHrMtFqoGObVTDxda5VfwEh_VbHQ
Jay M (1992) "the aesthetic ideology" as ideology; or, what does it mean to aestheticize politics? Cult Crit 21:41–61
Luciano G (1972) The concept of hegemony in Gramsci. Themelio, Athens, Greece
Mandoki K (2007a) Everyday aesthetics: prosaics, the play of culture and social identities. Ashgate, Aldershot
Mandoki WCI (1991) Estética y Poder. Dissertation. Universidad Nacional Autónoma de México
Mandoki K (1992) "El Poder de la Estética" In: *Arte y Coerción*. UNAM, México, pp 243–252
Mandoki K (2003) Terror and aesthetics: Nazi strategies for mass organisation. In: Roger Griffin (ed.) Critical concepts in political science. Routledge
Mandoki K (2007b) La construcción estética del estado y de la identidad nacional. Siglo Veintiuno editors, México D.F.
Mandoki K (2008) Retórica del cuerpo: en memoria de aquel hombre de Chang'an. En Helena Beristáin y Gerardo Ramírez Vidal (comp.) El cuerpo, el sonido y la imagen. UNAM, México, pp 11–21
Mandoki K (2015) The aesthetization of power; everyday aesthetics in nation states. In: Sebastian Stankiewicz (ed.) Transacting aesthetics. Jagellonian University, Krakow, pp 199–205
Mandoki K (2019) Letters on the aesthetic deformation of man. Contemporary Aesthetics. Online
Rancière J (2004) The politics of aesthetics. Continuum, London-New York
Rancière J (2005) From politics to aesthetics? Paragraph 28(1):13–25
Rancière J (2010) Dissensus: on politics and aesthetics. Continuum, London New York
Sartwell C (2010) Political aesthetics. Cornell University Press, Ithaca and London
Schiller F (1795) Letters upon the aesthetic education of man. http://public–library.uk/ebooks/55/76.pdf. (Accessed May 14, 2019)
Sontag S (1975) Fascinating fascism. The New York Review of Books. Feb 6
Spotts F (2009) Hitler and the power of aesthetics. Overlook Press, Woodstock and New York

Katya Mandoki is a retired Professor of Aesthetics and Semiotics at Universidad Autónoma Metropolitana in Mexico City. She initiated the systematic philosophical study of everyday aesthetics through both positive and negative aesthetic categories from a pragmatist philosophical and evolutionary perspective. Mandoki published eight books on this field: *Everyday Aesthetics; Prosaics, Social Identities and the Play of Culture* (Routledge, Ashgate 2007), *The Indispensable Excess of the Aesthetic: Evolution of Sensibility in Nature* (Rowman & Littlefield 2015, Spanish Siglo XXI 2013), *La construcción estética del Estado y de la identidad nacional; Prosaica III* (Siglo XXI 2007), *Prácticas estéticas e identidades sociales; Prosaica II* (Siglo XXI 2007), *Estética cotidiana y juegos de la cultura Prosaica I* (Siglo XXI 2006), *Estética y comunicación: de acciónpasión y seducción* (Norma 2006), *Prosaica; introducción a la estética de lo cotidiano* (Grijalbo 1994) and more than 200 papers related to this topic.

Political Concepts as Aesthetic Concepts

Max Ryynänen

Abstract Could it be, that when we think that we are using political concepts, the main accent could still, in some cases and/or situations, be cultural—or even aesthetic? This article outlines a reading of political discourse that invites us to think of the hidden cultural/aesthetic meaning of it. When one says'green' or'leftist', how often is one's focus on the practical agenda of politics—and how often is one thinking about the cultural tribe working on it? The political might also, in some cases, be just an instrument for an aesthetic agenda. And aesthetics might color political concepts in various ways.

Keywords Aesthetics · Politics · Aesthetic concepts · Political concepts · Party politics · The culture of politics · Political culture · Crispin Sartwell · Activism

Someone walks in and says that they hate The Green Party. For sure, on occasion, someone hates the ecological thinking or the social concerns of the party, but more often than not, the object of hate is a group of people, or a whole (sub)culture with shared aesthetic traits (hippies, hipsters, etc.). Concepts hide connotations and as such political concepts hide cultural and aesthetic implications.

In Finland, research shows that we are not more politically divided than what we used to be—politics here referring to e.g. economy, immigration and human rights. (It is actually the opposite: see Fornaro 2021) Still party politics has become more aggressive. Polarization and tribalization is fierce. In the US many white, poor and rural people (who voted for Trump) feel that they have been"forgotten", that they are the last unprivileged group of people that can be mocked in TV programs and that they do not exist in political discourse (Hochschild 2018). An overview of the cultural side of politics is needed and this book as a whole is intended to answer questions about the culture of politics. My choice, here, is to focus on even more marginal issues, i.e. on the aesthetics of politics, and the aesthetic side of political concepts.

M. Ryynänen (✉)
Helsinki, Finland
e-mail: max.ryynanen@aalto.fi

I will sketch out a basic view of the aesthetic side of political life in part one of my article, "Aesthetics and Politics: Introducing the Topic", by giving examples of a variety of ways in which politics is manifested aesthetically, and then presenting some thoughts by contemporary thinkers on the topic (Novitz 1992; Sartwell 2010; Friberg 2019).

The second part: "More Than Aesthetic Concepts", broadens the view of Frank Sibley's (1959) classical work on aesthetic concepts by introducing Wittgensteinian ways of thinking about aesthetic sensitivity (Johannesen 1994) and by forming a wider way of seeing political concepts as icebergs, that are sometimes only superficially political. Upon examination they lift up broader cultural issues, including aesthetics. My attempt is, through this inquiry, to assimilate a new way of thinking with regards to some of our problems regarding political rhetoric, which we often interpret too one-sidedly. I believe that starting to see political concepts as aesthetic concepts and by understanding politics as an aesthetic endeavour could take us further in current understanding of both areas. It is not to defend the connection of aesthetics and politics, but to take it seriously, as we too often think of political speech as just a political speech, and not a serious holistic, cultural, even aesthetic discourse. This could provide a new understanding of political practice.

Aesthetics and Politics: Introducing the Topic

Fare il bagno nella vasca è di destra/Far la doccia invece è di sinistra/un paccchetto di Marlboro è di destra/di contrabbando è di sinistra/Ma cos'è la destra cos'è la sinistra.

Giorgio Gaber's song *Destra-Sinistra* (1994) carnivalises the codes associated with the right- and left-wing supporters in Italian culture. Gaber exaggerates the sign language and aesthetic 'tribal culture' of the political extremes. In the song, smoking Marlboro is portrayed as right-wing; smoking smuggled cigarettes is left-wing; taking a bath is right-wing; taking a shower is left-wing.

Gaber's song is a pastiche. But politics, like any form of human life, is *culture*, and all cultures are networks of signs and symbols. Furthermore and central to this article: all cultural formations are loaded with standardised aesthetic traits. Prominent thinkers like Arnold Berleant (2012) and Michele Maffesoli (1993) have convincingly showed how communities become attached following their shared aesthetics.

Political groups are unified through their clothes, hairstyles, and gestures. Their members are both unconsciously and consciously directed to form the DNA of the sign, symbol and language of their party. When I was young, in the early 1990s, and a member of the leftist party, I noticed that I did not fit the aesthetics of the party with my rap clothes, which were, at the time, seen as somehow representing commercial (right-wing) culture. As a member of the Feminist Party of Finland, I received a timid wish to wear pink and provide an upbeat rhetoric during the 2019 parliament elections, where I was candidate.

Men in black suits and big black cars signify right-wing politics (if not all politics) in most countries. Many leftist males are either culturally coded as hipsters or dusty echoes of Che Guevara and/or Karl Marx with their beards. In many countries, long hair associates them with green thinking, peace activism and/or left wing-politics. Strongly gendered office clothes land more on the right-wing females—Silvia Federici's (Federici 2004) work on commodifying the nature of female office workers lands on aesthetic differentiating of female bodies—and gender blurring is a game played out in the liberal left. Ultra conservatives and the extreme right-wing borrow stylistically from early 20th century fascism and Nazism with clean-cut side hairs and long, tight trenches.

Political fairy tales are semi-literary, even fictional. As much as the Nordic (welfare) far left fantasizes about an aggressive fascist police, which they can 'fight back'—the police force in my home country of Finland is relatively soft and democratic—the extreme right continues the Grimm tradition in their scary tales about immigrants and asylum seekers. The music played is not all about words, but style too. It is somehow a must in many left-wing meetings to have 'alternative' music, like punk classics and/or 'authenticity'-driven rock music—as much as more clean-cut discoesque pieces with a 'cocaine touch' is commonplace for the economically upbeat liberal right-wing, and local schlager music, at least to an extent, makes many conservative nationalists happy.

Sometimes these styles and manners do develop out of a need to build a sensual and stylistic consensus, but often they break out naturally, I think, from the complex webs of cultural connections hiding in the worldview. Like clusters of musical styles, appearances and use of everyday poetical language binds together skateboarders as much as punks in their youth cultures; politicians play games with looks, music, and discourse which gluing up communities.

If the cultural systems are in any way able to produce pleasure, as I think they are, it is quite obvious that aesthetic pleasure has a major role in some people's political stances and actions.

There is more to it. It is not just symbols, sign language and a clearly recognisable style and this must be considered. There is something less definable at stake in politics, whether we talk about activist and grass root action, political parties, or the countless professionals, who work in politics without a clear identification or attachment to a party, from lobbers to janitors.

There is artistry and art at stake. There are musical pieces composed and/or performed to support presidential candidates. Parties and political institutions order paintings about their leaders. E.g. the president of Finland always orders at least one portrait of themselves. Besides the art, the festival planning (applied for party rallies) made by professionals in lighting and design, and the poetical speeches, which are often written by professionals; there is also a shallower everyday aesthetics at stake whenever politics is played out. One could talk about micro-semiotics, signs and significations of hardly or just unconsciously noticeable properties and meanings of sites, appearances and situations, where we feel at home or which arouse our feeling of being in the right place (Tarasti 2000). But I believe (and will return to this later), that this could at least sometimes be discussed through aesthetic sensitivity too.

Interestingly, there are no scholarly works which analyse the art, design, and everyday aesthetics of politics in detail, although we find some excellent work done on the topic more broadly. Crispin Sartwell's book *Political Aesthetics* is a bright overview of the aesthetics of politics. Sartwell claims that "at their heart political ideologies, systems, and constitutions are aesthetic systems, multimedia artistic environments," (Sartwell 2010: 1), which is not a debatable claim. His work focuses, though, on quite obvious cases, like Mussolini's fascism and German Nazism of the first half of the 20th century, and the artistic work behind these phenomena (Leni Riefenstahl, Albert Speer; see e.g. Sartwell 2010: 15, 23–28), and then alternative subcultures, like punk music. Of the American attack/engagement in Iraq, during the second Gulf War, Sartwell examines the pulling down of Saddam's statue. (Sartwell 2010: 34–35). In the end, reading his book does not help much more, than the endless comments we hear in everyday political discussions about the way elections in the US are a performance event and/or that some people vote for certain politicians just because they are 'good looking'. Of course, as an example, Nazism provides us with very distinctive aesthetics, which partly came to exist following its leaders' artistic backgrounds (Hitler's painting, Goebbels career as a writer). But would it not be more interesting to understand how masses in democracies move in 'flocks' and through aesthetic constellations by more subtle, everyday aesthetics?

Sartwell claims that ideologies are aesthetic systems, and what I think he means, is that aesthetics is not just added to ideology to increase its attractiveness, but that aesthetics is an integral part of the growth and development of politics. Aesthetics is not a decoration of politics. It is an organic part of its functionality. Sartwell notes that "(a)esthetic values and political values are not identical. There is a difference, for example, between beauty and justice." (Sartwell 2010: 11). At the same time, Sartwell still wants to show the difficulties in distinguishing them in practice. i.e. in the practice of politics we are able to separate them just on a theoretical level.

In his critical reading of Sartwell's book, Carsten Friberg finds Sartwell's reading of aesthetics too narrow:

> Very traditionally he understand aesthetics to be about "the nature of art; aesthetic values, especially beauty and sublimity; standards of taste and aesthetic assessment; and mimesis or representation." Difficulties arise when he, for example, gives beauty, which is seen as the object longing, a significant role to play. Obviously longing may appear in many contexts and forms such as the "rich, strange, mysterious, bewilderingly complex, teeming, or incomprehensible," but it also leaves the questions on what it is that is rich, strange etc. What is it we are longing for? And what enables us to utter biased statements about beauty, like Sartwell does, such as the assertion that the modern bureaucratic state is ugly? Our longing can change, he admits, and this change is exactly what I would call a change in our sensorial cognition. (Friberg 2019: 12–13)

In his article, Friberg turns towards radical sensibilities and atmospheres, and then, eventually, to perception, interpretation, and awareness. I think these multilayered planes of aesthetics are more realistic as companions towards understanding the connection of aesthetics and politics. In my article, I will explore this type of thinking and focus on concepts. But I want to start by showing the extreme effects of politics in our aesthetic encounters.

In a less political, older, and more everyday-driven book, David Novitz, attempts to clarify how much can we practically apply new ways of thinking which were trendy in the postmodernist 1980s. *Boundaries of Art* (1992), which Sartwell oddly does not mention in his work, critically assesses many themes of overcoming modernity, which were often and without support, hailed as signs of a new era at the time. Politics often finds its way into Novitz's thinking. Novitz's political brand test is illuminative. Imagine that Adolf Hitler would have done all the deeds that Gandhi did—and vice versa. Would Gandhi's smile not look horrifying? And would Hitler not look clumsy, in a more sympathetic way? (Novitz 1992).

The test where the 'content' of these two people affects their 'appearances' shows how much we change our way of looking at phenomena when we have differing information about them. This knowledge-based interpretation of appearances shows how careful we have to be with looks. Even beauty and charm are sometimes connected to what we know politically. Immanuel Kant stressed how beauty should (or could) be separated from other aspirations, but honestly, most people would have a hard time judging a rose as beautiful, if Hitler had planted it. The same could be said of Speer's architectural projects, which are often considered bizarre. In another political context, I am convinced, they would have appeared bold and radical.

Novitz's book does not dive into the concepts we use. (Neither is this the case with Sartwell or Friberg.) As much as art talks, political talk is an integral part of the 'business'. Could political concepts offer us a flight into the problematics? It might be productive to start from the aesthetic concepts, as there is a discussion about their nature.

More Than Aesthetic Concepts

The discourse on aesthetic concepts was outlined in contemporary culture by Frank Sibley. In his classical article "Aesthetic Concepts" (1959), he discussed the issue from the perspective of analytic philosophy of language. He describes our use of concepts, pointing out that ones like red or straight are not aesthetic concepts, as they just point out properties.

Kant claimed, in his analytic of the beautiful, that we judge something as beautiful when we are convinced that someone else is able to see what we do, the beauty of it (Kant 1952: 94). According to Sibley (whose work echoes Kant's analytical understanding of the beautiful), aesthetic concepts are what we use when we try to point out something in a work, something that is otherwise hard to grasp. Following this 'pointing out', someone may be able to see what we see.

It is too easy to say that an object or a painting is red, and this takes no perception and understanding of an art work further. In addition, there is no need then to use complicated concepts, but by pointing out that the structure of a poem is very 'intense' or that a film is 'touching' is something which pushes for more depth of understanding, into more obscure waters. Sibley wants us to really focus on the difference between totally aesthetic use and use which could be mostly about plain perception. He actually says that the concepts we use for aesthetics are also existing outside of art, that they are not always used in an aesthetic sense—although he notes, too, that some concepts (like beautiful) are always aesthetic, in and outside of art. He does not mention other cultural structures which could be connected more marginally to the aesthetic side of our lives, as he is following Kant's idea of aesthetics (and art) as a purist enterprise, differentiating it from other issues, which narrows down its meaning to e.g. roses and European tradition of painting.

Sibley claims that many people do not have this sensitivity for aesthetics. This sounds a bit too radical. He might mean that they do not have the sensitivity for Western highbrow art, and I do not think he would be opposed to Sartwell's or Friberg's ideas on the everyday nature of aesthetics, although he might have used different terms to discuss them. But one could say that he would not consider everyday politics as a field of aesthetics, as aesthetics there is not purified and autonomic, like it is in Western art. He would, perhaps, accept a formally beautifully painted image of Muhammad Gaddafi as beautiful, which would have disturbed many in the political and aesthetic disciplines, if it would have been presented in the art scene in the right context. More importantly, could you imagine anyone who would be totally aesthetically numb?

In a kind of a Wittgensteinian response to this, Kjell S. Johannesen discusses the way encounters with art are connected to a sensitivity, something acquired, something we are trained to notice, understand and enjoy. Harmony in music is a good example, or balance in a picture. These are sensitivities we learn by training. Similar to Sibley's ideas, it probably helps when someone tells us the facts verbally at some point in our development, if we want to be able to use a sensitivity. i.e. if no one ever told me when a piece of music or a chord sounds harmonic, could I have ever gained the point of it?

I'd like to build upon these two ideas: One is Sibley's sharp note that aesthetic concepts are used to point something (hardly perception based) out. Another one is Johannesen's way of talking about our sensitivities. What if we learned politics partly through aesthetic notes by our peers, both in Sibley's and the Wittgensteinian way? I think it is reasonable to believe that Sartwell is right here, when he claims that in practice, aesthetics is a part of political activity, and only clearly separable when analysed.

I think it is very seldom when culture and aesthetics take over politics, but this might have been the case for some sections of Fascists or Nazis. But what I think is that political concepts can sometimes be surprisingly aesthetically laden. To me, it looks like aesthetics often land heavily in concepts we consider to be political, not mostly dominating them, but staying often connotative or just marginally included in them, but sometimes suddenly being on the front of their meaning for a moment.

A colleague of mine said that he hates activism. He gave examples about dirty hippies with safe middle-class backgrounds, preparing vegetarian food and repairing bicycles in squatted houses, and playing punk music. The remark takes us to the core of a culture, not what activism means as a phenomenon in a hardcore political or pragmatic sense.

One could encounter this 'critique' by saying that this is just a cultural thing, and that activism itself is a pragmatic, action-based phenomena. Furthermore, it could be argued that there is a huge difference between the performative hobby activists in art schools (not all art school activists are of course like this) and Greenpeace activists who endanger their lives out at sea. The word activist might often be used about people who are more into this cultural label than the practical work. Working in the arts, I see that the word activism has really lost its edge, as many people who just take part in the cultural action by hanging out in the 'circles' or writing political comments on Facebook, have really left a mark on the concept.

It is not that I would say that the activists who are dominantly just part of the culture would dominate the practice of people we call activists; but that for many who gaze at the phenomenon from a distance, the visible part might be this less politically impactful middle class culture of wannabe revolution. This is unfair for those who use activism to change the world. The same problem applies to political parties. The most populist and stylistically distinguishable party members leave too much of a trace of the culture and aesthetics of politics on their parties, which is sad for those who concentrate just on the practical work of e.g. economic and/or social change. Some political tribes and individuals are active with their visible 'style', more than what they are with practical content. Aesthetics, not the lack of it (which to some extent defines bureaucracy), is on the front. Most political work, action, and thinking blurs these two aspects of politics.

There are moments, when oscillating between the political and the aesthetic, experience leans more to the aesthetic side, whether we'd want it or not. After seeing a rude situation produced by a certain identifiable group, one easily connects it to the whole group and its agenda. The situations which we remember somehow touch us. There are moments when political chaos, multitasking, and experiential looseness suddenly gathers its energies and one acknowledges 'an experience', to borrow John Dewey's (Dewey 1934) words. Good examples of this include idealistic rallies and disappointments in watching the political action of people representing a certain party. These moments as intensified experiences matter, and it is easy to see that many of the world's leading parties and leaders do everything they can to create political 'experiences' as events as beautifully, charmingly, extatically as possible.

The same applies to concepts, as mentioned earlier. The ex-leader of the Finns party, Timo Soini, discussed 'bicycle communism' a couple of years ago. I think the concept was related to an image of someone with counter culture clothes using a Christiania bike—cycling around in a trendy self-centered way, happy about the feeling of moral righteousness they exhibited. It was symbolic exaggeration, but I felt that there was a cultural judgement behind it; one where politics divided into experiential, cultural, and aesthetic understanding.

By taking up a 'fat union man', one paints rhetorically and ironically a sketch about what one in many countries sees as the old male social democrat. In someone's mind, Social Democracy might not anchor to the long days politicians work to design new laws or read reports, but to an atmosphere created by the middle-aged males with grumpy union suits who you don't see in other parties.

Atmospheres and sensual traces can stay around for years and stem from very small sensitivities, just as they rise from the mass sensually enough. Thus, it may be this appearance of politics where it seems at its strongest, the picturesque (to twist the word), the peculiar which lands in the field of meaning of concepts, like leftist or right-wing. Although most greens dress like 'anyone', the morally upbeat Jesus-type steals the show.

I could imagine an art critic writing about politics, and how this work would make us more conscious about the aesthetic side of politics. While this is something which has not to my knowledge been researched, I do believe that analysing the aesthetic sides of politics could teach us to understand politics better. While appearances in politics meet interpretations, which are based on our knowledge (Gandhi/Hitler), it is interesting to think how much appearances also dominate the concepts we use about politics.

The whole party has its own appearance. As I wrote about my experience of representing the Feminist Party in the elections, someone at the 'cigar level' of the party (in my marginal party just a small group of active people), works hard on the concepts, colours and ways of presenting the party, which leave an imprint on the whole activity. These strategies are already based on traditions (red for the left and the unions etc.), but new cultural formations appear on the stage every year.

Sometimes the appearance is about form and content, as our Hitler/Gandhi example shows. Sometimes it is a subtle sensitivity of what is done, how, and when—or how the order (visual, sensual) is constructed organically by the community. What happens in aesthetic sensitivity is much more complex, ranging from harmonies to microscopic meanings to styles of gesturing, which we all slowly learn through training.

The long history we have in art research, criticism, and aesthetics might help us to turn our focus on politics itself. A good analysis and education of this perspective to the broader masses (like biologists help us to understand climate change) clarifies what is not appearance, interpretation of appearance, or a shared sensitivity i.e. what politics is when it is beyond aesthetics.

We need good, rich descriptions of political events and situations in the style of Arnold Berleant's "descriptive aesthetics", where the philosopher aspires to write rich and pornographically detailed descriptions of his life to understand its aesthetic value (Berleant 1995: 25–39). We truly need to see beyond aesthetics, and here, I think I agree with Sartwell about the challenge to this. Yet the experts could make a change here by helping out the people who do politics but do not have the time to focus on its language and conceptual dimension, I am sure.

It is interesting that we fight for true facts and talk about post-truth at the same time as we do not challenge our aesthetics of politics, which colours our opinions and makes us partially see things. Everything is not just about semiotics. As much as lies, aesthetics can mislead content, often not in a radical way, but smoothly, shifting the focus, through lurking in our words and conceptions. When people look like you, talk like you, and act like you, others become your opponents, opponents of the flock, a differing tribe. Becoming one with the appearance in politics could be a dangerous way of drifting into being more aesthetical than political in content; an issue we all must face and challenge.

Political concepts reflect this, and as politics, besides images, is a lot about (endless) talk (like art is), grabbing the political concepts, which are also to some extent aesthetic concepts, might be the best start on the way to purify politics from needless aesthetics, at least theoretically, so that we could see more and understand better. Whether this project would lead to a rewriting of the language of politics, is an issue yet to be discussed.

References

Berleant A (1995) The aesthetics of environment. Temple University Press, Philadelphia
Berleant A (2012) Aesthetics beyond the arts: new and recent essays. Ashgate, Aldershot
Federici S (2004) Caliban and the witch: women, the body and primitive accumulation. Autonomedia, New York
Fornaro P. (2021) Onko suomalainen politiikka polarisoitunut? ETLA, Helsinki
Friberg C (2019) Political aesthetics. a philosophical reflection. Popular Inquiry 4:9–25
Hochschild AR (2018) Strangers in their own land. The New Press, New York, p 2016
Johannesen KS (1994) Kunst, språk og estetisk praksis. Uppsala Universitet, Uppsala
Kant I (1952) The critique of judgement. Clarendon Press, Oxford
Maffesoli M (1993) La contemplation du monde. Grasset, Paris
Novitz D (1992) Boundaries of Art. Temple University Press, Philadelphia
Sartwell C (2010) Political aesthetics. Cornell University Press, Ithaca
Sibley F (1959) Aesthetic concepts. Philos Rev 68:421–450
Tarasti E (2000) Existential Semiotics. Indiana University Press, Bloomington

Max Ryynänen is Senior Lecturer of Theory of Visual Culture and Head of the MA program Visual Culture and Contemporary Art in Aalto University (Helsinki/Espoo). He is the Editor-In-Chief of *The Journal of Somaesthetics* (with Richard Shusterman and Falk Heinrich) and *Popular Inquiry: The Journal of the Aesthetics of Kitsch, Camp and Popular Culture* (with Jozef Kovalcik). His late books include e.g. *On The Philosophy of Central European Art: The History of an Institution and Its Global Competitors* (Lexington Books, 2020), *Aesthetics in Dialogue* (Peter Lang, 2020, ed. with Zoltan Somhegyi) and *Art, Excess, and Education* (Palgrave, 2019, ed. with Kevin Tavin and Mira Kallio-Tavin). Currently he is editing *Cultural Approaches to Disgust and the Visceral* for Routledge together with Susanne Ylönen and Heidi Kosonen. http://maxryynanen.net.

Care as Key to Political Aesthetics

Elisabetta Di Stefano

Abstract The paper investigates the concept of care starting from Socrates and Plato to Italian Humanism, as the art of educating ourselves and others to live a good life. Taking into account some contemporary philosophical perspectives (Richard Shusterman; Yuriko Saito; Ellen Dissanayake) the author focuses on care in relation to the notion of sensitiveness, education and community. Then she claims that care has a key role within political aesthetics, understanding aesthetics as "theory of perception", in line with the German philosopher Alexander Baumgarten.

Keywords Care · Artification · Somaesthetics · Decorum · Education · Political aesthetics

Introduction

According to the myth narrated by Plato in the *Statesman* (274 b–d; 1995), there was a time when the gods decided to no longer provide man with any guidance or support. They then left man alone, with no protection, means or resources, to live together with ferocious beasts to the peril of his life. However, before abandoning him, the gods gave man the arts (*téchnai*) so as to enable him to take care (*epimèleia*) of himself alone. As we know, from ancient culture to Renaissance the notion of art (*téchne* in Greek; *ars* in Latin) identified a very wide range of manual and intellectual activities which improved the life of the people (Tatarkiewicz 1980).

Based on this myth, since the arts involve the collaboration among those who have knowledge, the arts have provided the ground for our social and political life. Unlike other arts which yield a specific product, politics finds its purpose by bringing order in the relationships of mutual cooperation, in other words, harmonizing contrasts and excesses in view of the preservation of the common good. In the *Statesman*, the importance granted to ethical ends and education leads Plato to repeatedly define

---

E. Di Stefano (✉)
Palermo, Italy
e-mail: elisabetta.distefano@unipa.it

politics, within a breeding metaphor (261d; 268a), as the art of taking care (*epimèleia*) of mankind (*Statesman* 276c).

The notion of care is often connected to politics by Plato. In the *First Alcibiades* (124 a–b) one reads that self-care (*epimèleia heautoù*) is a self-educating practice: it is a way to improve oneself as much as possible to prepare for public life (128a–e). In fact, in order to qualify for any office, it is deemed necessary to prove one's ability for caring for others (*epimèleia*). In this dialogue, Plato refers to Socrates' theory according to which care is an art (*téchne*) that can be taught and learnt (118d). Care is not self-referential, but in relation to others, so as to help them in turn to take care of themselves. In this regard, care is the art of educating others to fully express themselves according to human and political virtues (Plato, *Apology of Socrates*, 20b; 1995), on the assumption that only a good life, based on the study and practice of virtue, makes us fully human and good citizens, as well as making life worth living.

On this premise, I will investigate the concept of care taking into account both some historical roots as well as contemporary philosophical perspectives (Richard Shusterman; Yuriko Saito; Ellen Dissanayake), highlighting differences and common points. Furthermore, I will argue in favor of its key role within political aesthetics. Needless to say, aesthetics is here not to be understood as a philosophy of art, but as the "theory of perception", as outlined by the German philosopher Alexander Baumgarten. In the 18th century, Baumgarten came up with the name *Aesthetica* (from the Greek word *aisthesis*) for a new branch of philosophy investigating sensitiveness. The latter is thereby credited a knowledge value analogous to that of reason (Baumgarten 1954). According to Baumgarten, whereas intellectual knowledge relies on signs (i.e. language, mathematics, etc.) which makes it abstract and inactive, sense-based knowledge has the ability to translate itself into action. This pragmatic key is however alien to main stream aesthetics, such as the one developed on Kant's "disinterestedness". This is why Baumgarten's theory provides a suitable basis for political aesthetics, giving tools to develop the sense-based knowledge useful in everyday experience and making life actually good for oneself and for the whole community.

Self-Care as the "Art of Living"

The ancient idea of care as the art of educating oneself and others on human and political virtues resounds over Italian Humanism which interprets classical culture as an ethic and civic engagement (Garin 1965). A remarkable revival of the notion of self-care can be found in Francesco Petrarch's works. Some of his writings (*Secretum*; *Familiares* I, 9) aim to shape oneself as an ethical subject through techniques of self-cultivation like reading salutary texts and writing notes to memorize precepts of virtuous conduct (Zak 2014: 217–240). As Zak points out, Leon Battista Alberti further expands this Petrarchan ideal by considering the care of the body, by means of physical exercises, an integral part of his process of self-care. In his autobiographical *Vita* (1438) Alberti describes his habit of constantly observing his own conduct, examining in particular the way he walks in the street, rides a horse, and speaks. Furthermore, he describes a list of physical exercises he usually did, stressing that he performed these exercises to keep fit (playing ball, the use of the javelin with thong, running, wrestling and climbing steep mountains). Later in his vernacular dialogue *Della Famiglia* (*On the family*) the care of oneself becomes the cornerstone of household and family management. In Book 1, while discussing the education of children, it is said that the father has to care for his children by training both their body and soul («Exercise, then, is very useful not only for the body but for the soul» Alberti 1971: 70). Furthermore, in his dialogue *Profugiorum ab erumna* (*On refuge from hardships*), the "care of the soul" based on exercise and experience is presented as the central goal of living; consequently, we can affirm that for Alberti the care of the soul and body is a philosophy of life that takes place «in the midst of men in the city's squares» (Zak 2014: 227–237).

Up to today the notion of care is one of the pillars of pedagogical studies. In this regard, self-knowledge and self-care are not merely introspectively understood, but taken as "questioning the self in relation to the world one inhabits", in other words, taking into account the relationships and situations one experiences (Mortari 2008: 52).

As soon as self-care is understood as a practice in a relational space, it acquires not only a pedagogical value, but also a political one. Along these lines, it is my intention to develop an argument in support of the aesthetics of care, that is, care grafted on the theory of sensitive knowledge (Baumgarten 1954), that unlike symbolic and speculative knowledge, it is able to translate itself into action and practical application (*Aesthetica* § 70; *Metaphysica* § 669–671).

In the theoretical framework of pragmatist aesthetics this efficiency of sensitive knowledge has been further developed by Richard Shusterman, who advocates care of the self as the "art of living", also known as somaesthetics (Shusterman 1999 e 2012). By focusing on the notion of *soma* ("living body"), Shusterman aims at re-establishing the human psycho-physical integrity and supports its conscious spreading in our environment, daily practices and relations: «Concerned not simply with the body's external form or representation but also with its lived experience, somaesthetics works at improving awareness of our bodily states and feelings, thus providing greater insight into both our passing moods and lasting attitudes. It can therefore reveal and improve somatic malfunctionings that normally go undetected even though they impair our wellbeing and performance» (Shusterman 1999: 302–303). As it draws attention to bodily experiences affecting and shaping our bodies according to cultural norms and social conventions, Shusterman's theory has a great biopolitical spillover. Among his authors of reference, one finds indeed Michel Foucault, who, in *Discipline and Punish: The Birth of the Prison*, investigated the somatic implications of the surveillance regime and of prison detention. Later on, in *The History of Sexuality*, Foucault also pointed out the forms of repression of sexuality in many systems of power (Shusterman 2000: 530–551).

As it favors the development of bodily awareness, somaesthetics can improve the quality of daily life in terms of health and wellbeing. This is what Shusterman defines as the "art of living": not an aestheticized life, the pursuing of a merely external, superficial, and consumeristic beauty, but a life worth living, that is to say, being at ease with oneself and others, based on the bodily awareness that leads to a healthier and more performant body in every situation.

This somaesthetic strategy, as Shusterman points out, has ancient philosophical roots. It is not a coincidence that Shusterman refers precisely to Socrates as to the founder of a theoretical and practical philosophy revolving around the care of the self and the achievement of psycho-physical integrity: «Socrates himself affirmed the crucial role of somatic care, and "took care to exercise his body and kept it in good condition" by regular dance training and simple living. "The body," he declared, "is valuable for all human activities, and in all its uses it is very important that it should be as fit as possible. Even in the act of thinking, which is supposed to require least assistance from the body, everyone knows that serious mistakes often happen through physical ill-health» (Shusterman 1999: 302; Diogenes Laertius 1991: 153, 163).

From Socrates to Cyrenaic Aristippus, from Zeno—father of Stoicism—to Diogenes—founder of Cynicism—many ancient Greek philosophers advocated somatic training in pursuit of wisdom and virtue, considering philosophy as a "way of living" (Hadot 1995). The emphasis on the care for both body and soul was also a dominant theme in Quattrocento humanism, as we have already seen, and as Vergerio's treatise on education confirms: «Because a person is composed of soul and body, those to whom strength of body and intellect has been given seem to me to have gained some things great from nature […] The thanks that are due to nature, moreover, will be paid if we have not neglected her gifts but rather taken care to cultivate them through the right sort of studies in the liberal arts» (Kallendorf 2002: 8–9).

Through the history of ideas we can understand that over the centuries, despite the differences connected with the cultural background, the notion of self-care is a way of educating oneself and others as ethical and political subjects aiming to live a good life within the community.

Care as Appropriateness

Moving from a different philosophical background, the Japanese–American scholar Yuriko Saito provides an important contribution to the notion of care. Long acknowledged as the founding mother of the philosophical stream named after her famous book, *Everyday Aesthetics* (2007), Saito can also be seen as a supporter of an «Aesthetics of Care» (Iannilli 2019: 103; Saito 2020).

The noun "care" and the adjective "carefully" occur frequently in Saito's book, especially in the final chapter focusing on moral-aesthetic judgments regarding everyday artifacts and man-built environments (Saito 2007: 205). As Saito explains: «They are judgments of moral virtues, such as care, considerateness, sensitivity, and respect, or lack thereof, made on artifacts and built environments on the basis of their perceptual features resulting from design. Although inseparable from the functional value, moral-aesthetic judgments go beyond it by appraising the way in which the care and respect for the materials, users, and dwellers are embodied, expressed, or reflected in the choice of materials and their arrangements» (Saito 2007: 7). According to her, care is particularly important in planning objects and buildings for people with "special needs" «such as the physically challenged, children, senior citizens, sick patients, and displaced refugees. In designing objects and spaces for people with "special needs," we cannot but become sensitive and responsive to their specific interests and capacities». As she points out that designing for people like this «we attend carefully not only to the size, shape, texture, color, and safety of the objects but also to less tangible factors, ranging from comfort and well-being to the potential for discrimination, marginalization, cultural displacement, social stigma, and the like» (Saito 2007: 219), Saito's aesthetics of care acquires political value.

Focusing on «the care and respect for the materials, users, and dwellers», Saito echoes the notion of appropriateness or adaptedness to purpose which had already been developed in the classical era through the ancient Greek word *prepon* (Pohlenz 1933) and the Latin *decorum* (Cicero, *Orator* 21, 70: «The Greeks call it *prepon*; let us call it *decorum*, or 'propriety'»). *Decor* and *decorum* mean the "pertinence" of something in relation to an established objective both in ancient rhetoric (Cicero; Quintilian) and architecture (Vitruvio); they do share a common root with the impersonal verb *decet* ("it is fitting") which entails a reference to the ethical and social realm. Ranging from philosophy and rhetoric to design and good manners the notion of appropriateness is line with the "aesthetics of care" that Saito points out in relation to designed objects and social interaction (Saito 2020: 193–199).

Without referring to the idea of care, the notion of appropriateness has been focused on by Glenn Parsons and Allen Carlson and later by Jane Forsey. In the contemporary anglo-american debate, while retrieving the Greek concept of "fitness" (*prepon*) to find a historical support to the claims of "functional beauty", Parsons and Carlson (2008: 2–4) venture into the question of whether beauty results from "being fit" or "looking fit" for function. They thus forget that, according to the rhetoric theory of *prepon/decorum*, there is no dyscrasia between the two options. Both Aristotle and Cicero (*De or*.: III, 45, 179) conceive the perfection of the discourse on the model of the human body, that is beautiful because each organ fits its specific function. Following the rhetoric tradition, the architect Leon Battista Alberti compares buildings to living organisms («a building is very like an animal»; Alberti 1988: IX, 5, 301), and on this ground points to the unity of "being" fitting to purpose and "looking" fitting to purpose: «Take the case of a horse: they realized that the shape of each member looked suitable for a particular use, so the whole animal itself would work well in that use. Thus they found that grace of form could never be separated or divorced from suitability for use» (Alberti 1988: VI, 3, 158). The correspondence between external appearance and purpose in buildings is expressed by Alberti in reference to a royal palace and a tyrant's fortress. The shape of two types of architecture mirrors different "characters", related to their respective political strategies (Alberti 1988: V, 3, 121–122). Without mentioning rhetoric but staying in the same line, Jane Forsey (2013: 238) connects the idea of function with those of "character" and "active use": «The functional beauty [...] marks out its everyday character, which can be experienced only through active use as demanding singular and specific attention».

To understand more clearly the relation between the notion of appropriateness and that of care, we can do an excursus through the ancient texts. In the Platonic dialogue, *Hippias Major* (289d–290e), talking about utensils, Socrates claims that not all materials are well adapted to all shapes, but only to those for which they are "appropriate". Socrates' lesson can then be seen as a "sort of everyday aesthetics", inasmuch as it includes household objects (the wooden spoon, the garbage bin), as well as military ones, where the use of appropriate material has decisive consequences on the safety and comfort of its users. In a passage from Xenophon's *Memorabilia* (III, 8, 4), Socrates claims that a golden shield, although beautiful to look at, is not suited to a battle since gold is too fragile to guarantee safety. The careful choice of materials then translates into care for the people who are going to use them and for their needs. This is clearly stated in a later section of the *Memorabilia* (III, 10, 9–13). Talking to the armorer, Pistias, who is bragging about his breastplates and how they are well-made because they are well-proportioned, Socrates claims that an armor should not be perfectly well-proportioned, but in relation to the wearer (Xenophon 1979: 237–239).

While varying from objects of use to dwellings (*Memorabilia* III, 8, 8–10), Socrates highlights the notion of appropriateness to purpose that focuses on people and their needs. Within this context Yuriko Saito's thoughts find a fitting place, in my opinion. Clearly, over the centuries the category of *decorum* underwent several transformations in relation to different philosophical backgrounds. In Saito's reasoning for instance, the care for the materials, the users, and the inhabitants is enriched with perceptual and sensorial nuances previously unheard of, especially in the aesthetic debate before the 18th century. She thinks that bodily sensations are extremely important as they are a barometer for our health and safety, ultimately determining the quality of life. According to Saito, buildings and objects should not be designed based on merely aesthetic criteria (materials, shapes, decorations) nor based on merely functional ones (intended use); on the contrary, it is important to take care of people and respect them while imagining the psychological and physical reactions that objects and environments will produce on their users (Saito 2017: 227). To take care of the users means taking into account their wellbeing in connection with the feeling of comfort or discomfort that environments trigger in those who inhabit them, inasmuch as these feelings can have a positive or negative impact on one's mood, professional performance, and even on one's health.

Connecting the field of buildings and good manners, unconsciously in line with the notion of *decorum*, Saito polemicizes against the narcissistic and self-referential trends in contemporary architecture, which make it arrogant if not alienating and, following Juhani Pallasmaa (1999), she wishes for «an architecture of courtesy and attention» (Saito 2007: 221).

In origin courtesy would stand for the respect of given rules of conduct and being endowed with certain virtues (e.g. kindness, generosity) which used to be a prerequisite for members of the court. Furthermore, as Baldesar Castiglione (1901, par.

7–8, 82–83) says, the perfect courtier must show courtesy and most of all "discretion"—that is to say, the ability to act appropriately according to circumstances—an essential skill in social and political life.

In a leap from the Renaissance to the present time, within the line of the notion of appropriateness applied to political and social behaviors, the remarks regarding tact presented by another supporter of Everyday Aesthetics, Ossi Naukkarinen, find an appropriate collocation. Tact is a natural endowment linked to the category of discretion and the realm of good manners. The Finnish scholar claims that tact is to be understood as a behavioral mode which is appropriate to given circumstances and respectful of others. To behave tactfully is really important in all sectors where a given behavioral etiquette is in place (e.g. at work; in politics; in social relations). In the globalized and multiethnic world of today, it is easy to crash against customs stemming from different cultural values and behavioral norms. In this context, to use tact means to follow a form of sensibility related to the situation, selecting actions based on circumstances (Naukkarinen 2014). In short, following Władysław Tatarkiewicz' (1980) example, courtesy and tact would be inscribed in the same historical path of appropriateness.

While laying emphasis on the importance of courtesy, adaptedness to purpose, and care, Yuriko Saito faces the difficult task to assign an aesthetic value to moral qualities. However, by resorting to the history of ideas, a way out is provided from the apparent conflict between aesthetics and ethics. Over the centuries—from Leon Battista Alberti to the European Romanticism, from Louis H. Sullivan to the organic architecture movement (Di Stefano 2012, 2019)—the notion of appropriateness has stood for an ethical and aesthetic measure in design, contrasting merely aesthetic trends (a beautiful appearance) or strictly functional ones.

Furthermore, the history of ideas of appropriateness provides a fruitful contribution to outlining how care can work as a key element in political aesthetics. This happens by taking into account how objects and environments have an impact on the users' perception and quality of life. Inspite of their good intention, most of the time architects and designers don't actually manage to reach an "architecture of good manners", in line with Tristan Edward's teaching (Edward 1944). Why is this? An answer may be found in a technological and scientific education lacking human disciplines like psychology, sociology, anthropology, and aesthetics (understood as the theory of sensitiveness). It is not a coincidence that many of those who promote a "design that takes care of people" don't have a "scientific" education. One of those is the psychologist Donald Norman, who affirms: «Good design takes care» because «it takes conscious attention to the needs of the user» (Donald 1990: 25). With the help of his wife who is a psychologist, the Danish architect Jan Gehl has focused his career on improving the quality of urban life, planning cities that are lively, safe, sustainable, and healthy (Gehl 2010; 2011). Aware of how city planning influences public life, Gehl advocates a sensitive approach that looks after people and their needs carefully taking into account the five human senses.

It is worth remembering that in the sixties, following Hermann Helmholtz' famous speech (*The Relation of the Natural Sciences to Science in General*, 1862), Gadamer pointed out that human sciences have no method of their own, but they have other not logical tools, like tact: «By "tact" we understand a special sensitivity and sensitiveness to situations and how to behave in them, for which knowledge from general principles does not suffice» (Gadamer 2004: 14). Because «the tact which functions in the human sciences is not simply a feeling and unconscious, but is at the same time a mode of knowing and a mode of being» (Gadamer 2004: 15), an education aiming at raising sensitive knowledge is crucial for political aesthetics.

Care as "Making Special"

Care for small things in everyday life is common practice in the Japanese culture, where each gesture, object and element of decoration has its own value within the sphere of relationships where aesthetics and morality are fused together. Yuriko Saito mentions some popular examples, such as the tea ceremony, the art of the garden, the presentation and the packaging of food. She does not fail to mention other cultures as well, such as the Navajos, the Balinese people and the Inuit people (Saito 2007: 41), for which artistic practices are an integral part of ordinary life, thus everyday life is geared towards an artistic sensibility: «In such cultures, everyone is an artist and every activity is an artistic activity in the sense that it is practiced with utmost care, skillful execution, and in pursuit of excellence and beauty» (Saito 2007: 4).

In this respect, Saito's aesthetics of care shares some features with the theory of "making special" advocated by the ethologist Ellen Dissanayake, given that both of them focus on the everyday rituals and on the value of taking care of what is special within a community. Dissanayake's studies are placed within the framework of evolutionary aesthetics in respect to which they offer an original perspective. In the essay *Homo Aestheticus* (1992) and in some subsequent studies Dissanayake investigates different human behaviors which can be found since the time of pre-historical societies—as for instance the need to sing, dance, tell stories and decorate objects—with the aim of identifying the origins of a "species-specific aesthetic sense". While moving away from the abstract and ethnocentric notion of art, elaborated in Europe between the 17th and the 19th century, she points out that «Art is a normal and necessary behavior of human beings» (Dissanayake 1992: 225). According to Dissanayake, «art—as we know it and as we recognize it in other human societies, present and past, even those which have no concept or word for art—is an instance of this broader human faculty or proclivity for making special. In its specifically artistic form it is concerned with shaping and embellishing everyday ordinary reality so that it becomes extraordinary, i.e., on a different "level" from the usual daily round of satisfying vital needs of food, rest, social interaction, shelter, care, and so forth» (Dissanayake 1982: 148).

Therefore, art is not the object of aesthetic contemplation, but a behavioral inclination which amounts to "making special" something, someone, or even actions themselves. For the first time in 2001 Dissanayake used the verb "artify" as a synonym for "making special" (Dissanayake 2013), as to convey the idea of making things "artfully"—with precision, attention to detail and the care for purpose. Artification is in this respect a practice of ordinary life with a transformative power. The power of making the ordinary extraordinary is in fact associated to ritual ceremonies in which gestures, objects, and behaviors stand for some biologically or socially relevant states with consequences on the community: «Ritual ceremonies are meant to affect biologically-important states of affairs that humans necessarily care about—assuring food, safety, health, fertility, prosperity, and so forth» (Dissanayake 2009: 156). Collective ceremonies help people find relief from anxiety in the uncertainties and dangers of life, inasmuch as rituals shape the emotions of the participants with beneficial effects on their individual fitness and on the cohesion of the community, strengthening their social bonds.

The notion of "making special" is linked to everything humans take more care of, like varnished utensils, weapons or objects that they use in a protective and effective way during ceremonies or particular events. Dissanayake takes the roots of this notion from the early affective relationship: the mother–infant interaction (Dissanayake–Miall 2003). Here simple daily actions, repeated, exaggerated, and elaborated, aim to express intense affection and communicate attentive reassurance and care: «In mother-infant interaction, the instrumental context for, say, touching is grooming and tending; for smiling it is showing relaxed pleasure. The other signals similarly also communicate friendliness or affiliation» (Dissanayake 2009: 155). Such a paradigmatic example clarifies to what extent the idea of making special is connected to care.

Finally, coming surprisingly close to Saito's remarks, Dissanayake recalls that in some societies, such as the Balinese one, people make each moment of the day special, in full awareness of the importance of small things: «when they care about something they are generally inclined to make it special. This is not to identify it (like yellow stars) or to indicate that it is specific (like a ribbon over auditorium seats reserved for distinguished guests)—but to show that one cares about it: "This treatment surpasses what is common or usual, because it has emotional relevance to me." I claim that it is an evolved feature of human psychology that when we care, we make special» (Dissanayake 2003: 11).

According to Dissanayake's theoretical assessment, making special has not only an honorific value but also an affective and cognitive one. It is the care, attention and effort put into doing something that has a particular value for the community which shows that these things are special; and it is this relational aspect that provides the concept of "making special" with a social and political value.

What is Political Aesthetics?

Before investigating in what respect the notion of care can provide a key contribution to political aesthetics, it is important to clarify what I understand as such. I do not intend to talk about the aestheticization of politics, that is to say, politics availing itself of staging actions. Naturally, in the process of "aestheticization of life" (Welsch 1997: 85–86), also the "political" is subdued to the logic of marketing and staging.

This process goes back to the 1930s, as the expression "aestheticization of politics" was first introduced by Walter Benjamin in reference to the symbolism of Fascism and Nazism, to the scenographic parades and public demonstrations, and more generally to the links among art, political propaganda and mass media (Benjamin 2003: 269–270).

On the contrary, the expression "Political Aesthetics" is more recent and has not yet received a clear definition. While choosing it for the title of one of his essays, Crispin Sartwell provides the following interpretation: «all politics is aesthetic; at their heart political ideologies, systems, and constitutions are aesthetic systems, multimedia artistic environments» (Sartwell 2010: 1). Such a definition, however, shows some weaknesses, inasmuch as it understands aesthetics as the romantic tradition did, in other words as «a subdiscipline of philosophy that is concerned [...] with four main questions (as well as many ancillary ones): the nature of art; aesthetic values, especially beauty and sublimity; standards of taste and aesthetic assessment; and mimesis or representation» (Sartwell 2010: 4–5). Taking distance from the romantic tradition and retrieving instead to the theory of sensitiveness (Baumgarten 1954), we can focus on the key role of sense-based knowledge and its educational outreach.

Also Ben Highmore focuses on the idea of political aesthetics in the last chapter of his book, *Ordinary lives*, titled *Towards a political aesthetics of everyday life*. Differently from Sartwell, he aims to highlight the «affective life of people», and «provide more sensual and phenomenological descriptions of social and cultural life» (Highmore 2010: 166). Highmore notably claims that: «The work of an aesthetic politics of the ordinary may be to produce imaginative acts for thinking the seemingly impossible: a culture that encourages habits of generosity and world-enlarging improvisation and adaptation, while also maintaining habits of comfort and stability» (Highmore 2010: 171).

As it is not tied to the art system and its aesthetic values (e.g. the beautiful, the sublime, taste, imitation), but rather focuses on daily practices based on a phenomenological and sensorial perspective, the notion of political aesthetics elaborated by Highmore presents greater advantages compared to Sartwell's. Interestingly, Highmore draws attention to some concepts, such as generosity, adaptation, and comfort, that are in line with the aesthetics of care suggested by Saito, but he does not develop his inquiry in this direction. He notably never connects these ethical and aesthetic concepts to the city understood as relational space, thus missing the opportunity to strengthen the proposal of political aesthetics.

The closest idea of political aesthetics to the one I am trying to focus on was outlined by the psychologist James Hillman. In his book *Politics of Beauty* (2005; but also in Hillman 2013) he traces back the word "Politics" to the Greek *pólis*, "city". Recalling the renaissance neoplatonic notion of *anima mundi* ("soul of the world") he means a city as a "tangible appearance of the soul of the community". Consequently, the care of the soul mustn't be understood as self-referential but concerning the world in which we live in, because only improving our city we improve ourselves. According to him, politics must be re-discovered in its original meaning as a cure capable of restoring the dignity of people and places respecting different traditions, customs and cultures, which is in line with the plurality that the word *pólis* (city) has from its root *Poli-*, "many" (Hillman 2005: 11–25). Hillman emphasizes the importance of dealing with things concerning the external world adopting a psychological perspective, attention to detail and individuality, and over all sensibility. Without referring to Baumgarten, he highlights an idea of *aisthesis*, understood as sensitiveness that makes individuals more conscious and capable of expressing themselves fully with a positive outcome for themselves and the whole community.

Developing further Hillman's perspective, I will now try to focus on the reason why Baumgarten's theory of sensitiveness can be a basis for political aesthetics in which the idea of care has a key role. According to Baumgarten, the aim of aesthetics is the perfection of sensitive knowledge (*Aesthetica* § 14). One of the paths leading to this perfection is the "life" of knowledge (*vita cognitionis*: *Aesthetica* § 22), that is to say, the ability that intuitive knowledge has in transforming itself into action and practical application (*Aesthetica* § 70; *Metaphysica* § 669–671). It is not a coincidence that Baumgarten refers to metaphors from the range of life ("fecund"; "pregnant") to give a physiological connotation to sense-based perception. As aptly emphasized by Salvatore Tedesco, Baumgarten presents the "body of argumentations"—in Aristotelian terms, *soma tes pisteos*—based on a «principle of form equipped with physiologically driving activity», which will be echoed also by vitalist medicine in the nineteenth century (Tedesco 2012: 8).

While attributing value to the kind of vitalism supported by Baumgarten, Shusterman's idea of self-care is to be understood not as a pursuit of external and superficial beauty, but as the "art of living". Making us aware that cultural, political and social norms affect our bodily habits, producing malfunctioning in our organs and having a negative psycho-physical influence, Shusterman's somaesthetics upholds the psychosomatic unity and its outcome in improving the quality of life in terms of health and wellbeing. By calling upon Socrates'idea of self-care and his notion of body fitness, he claims that somatic care produces bodily awareness that leads to a healthier and well performing body in each situation with positive consequence also on our relationships within a community.

The pragmatic potential of sensitiveness and its ability to transform into action are investigated also by Saito, even though she refers to Dewey's (1958) rather than to Baumgarten's theory. Interested in the architectural and object design, Saito places great emphasis on the notion of appropriateness and care of users and environments by taking into account the quality of life. This becomes particularly clear when Saito criticizes the search for beauty for its own sake and promotes a fitting behavior both ethically and aesthetically for the good of the community; consequently, it acquires a pedagogical and political value. According to Saito, «If we detect and appreciate that we are surrounded by objects and environments expressive of care and thoughtfulness, we tend to pass on kindness and consideration to those around us» (2017, 170). Good practices determine a "virtuous circle" from the environments to its inhabitants and back, triggering a series of processes which, adopting a medical metaphor, we can define as a form of "aesthetic contagion". Care therefore becomes the ethical and aesthetic criterion based on which a good and just society takes care of its citizens while in turn its citizens take care of the city.

Finally, according to the ethologist Dissanayake, artification makes objects or actions "special" and draws the attention of the viewers to them through ritual ceremonies. This "vividness" of artified objects, actions and bodies goes beyond the merely aesthetic realm and becomes "an acting and moving principle". This perspective seems in line with the anthropological theory of "agency" and "enchantment" (Gell 1998; 1992), according to which things have a "social life" and can act within a community (Appadurai 1986). Producing beneficial effects on individual fitness and on the cohesion of the community, also the notion of "making special" strengthens social bonds and acquires political value.

Conclusion

Starting from the ancient idea of care, from Socrates and Plato to the Italian Humanism, as the art to improve ourselves and others and live a good life, I have analyzed the theories of Shusterman, Saito and Dissanayake. While coming from different philosophical backgrounds (pragmatist aesthetics, everyday aesthetics, evolutionary aesthetics), they pointed out some notions (the art of living; the concept of appropriateness; the notion of "making special") that can be understood as care. Despite their different approach I have tried to highlight a *fil-rouge* pivoting on some key points: sensitiveness, education and community. Focusing on these ideas, I have tried to demonstrate that care can improve ourselves, others and our environment. Therefore, we can consider the notion of care as the key within political aesthetics if we understand it as questioning the self in relation to the city (*pólis*), and more generally to the world where we live, taking into account the relationships and situations we experience. Of course, we do not refer to aesthetics in terms of the aestheticization of life, as the production of a superficial and consumeristic-driven beauty, but rather, going back to Baumgarten, as the theory of sensitiveness (*aisthesis*). As the sense-based knowledge has the ability to transfer itself into action, Baumgarten's theory provides a suitable basis for political aesthetics, developing bodily awareness (*aisthesis*) useful in everyday experience. In this theoretical framework, the care of self and others acquires a political value, as it develops our ethical and civic virtues, leading us to responsible choices and making life worth living for ourselves and for the whole community.

References

Alberti LB (1971) The Albertis of Florence: LeonBattista Alberti's Della Famiglia. In: Guarino GA (transl.). Bucknell University Press, Lewisburg

Alberti LB (1987) Dinner pieces. In: David Marsh (transl.) Medieval & Renaissance Texts & Studies. Binghamton, New York

Alberti, LB (1988) On the art of building in ten books. In: Rykwert J, Leach N, Tavernor R (transl.). The MIT Press, Cambridge (Massachusetts)—London (England)

Appadurai A (ed) (1986) The social life of things: commodities in cultural perspective. Cambridge University Press, Cambridge

Baumgarten, AG (1954) Reflections on Poetry: Alexander Gottlieb Baumgarten's Meditationes philosophicae de nonnullis ad poema pertinentibus. In: Aschenbrenner K, Holther WB. University of California Press, Berkeley

Benjamin W (2003) Work of Art in the Age of Reproducibility. In: Jephcott E. (transl.) Selected Writings (1938–1940). The Belknap Press of Harvard University Press, Cambridge (Massachusetts)–London (England)

Castiglione B (1901) The Book of the Courtier. Leonard Eckstein Opdycke (transl.), Charles Scribner's Sons, New York

Cicero (1948) On the Orator, Books I–II (Loeb Classical Library No. 348). In: Sutton EW, Rackham H (transl.). Harvard University Press, Cambridge (Massachusetts)

Dewey J (1958) Art as Experience. Capricorn Press, New York

Dissanayake E (1982) Aesthetic experience and human evolution. J Aesthet Art CritIsm 41:145–155

Dissanayake E (1992) Homo aestheticus: where art came from and why. Free Press, New York

Dissanayake E (2003) Retrospective on homo aestheticus. J Can Assoc Curric Stud 1:7–11

Dissanayake E (2009) The artification hypothesis and its relevance to cognitive science, evolutionary aesthetics, and neuroaesthetics. Cogn Semiot 5:148–173

Dissanayake E (2013) Genesis and development of «Making Special»: is the concept relevant to aesthetic philosophy? Rivista Di Estetica 54:83–98

Dissanayake E, Miall DS (2003) The poetics of babytalk. Human Nat 14:337–64

Donald AN (1990) The design of everyday things. Doubleday, New York

Edwards AT (1944) Good and bad manners in architecture: an essay on the social aspects of civic design. John Tiranti, London

Elisabetta DS (2019) La convenance de l'ornement: une question éthique? Nouvelle revue d'esthétique 1:87–94

Elisabetta DS (2012) The aesthetic of Louis H. Sullivan: between ornament and functionality. In: Joerg Gleiter (ed.) Ornament Today. Bozen University Press, Bolzano, 64–75

Forsey J (2013) The aesthetics of design. Oxford University Press, Oxford

Gadamer HG (2004) Truth and Method. In: Joel W, Donald GM, 2nd revised ed. Continuum, London-New York

Garin E (1965) Italian humanism: philosophy and civic life in the renaissance. In: Peter Munz (transl.). Harper and Row, New York

Gehl J (2011) (1971 first ed.). Life between buildings: using public space. Island Press, Washington

Gehl J (2010) Cities for people. Island Press, Washington

Gell A (1992) The technology of enchantment and enchantment of technology. In: Coote J, Shelton A (eds.) Anthropology, Art and Aesthetics. Clarendon Press, Oxford

Gell A (1998). Art and agency. An anthropological theory. Clarendon Press, Oxford

Hadot P (1995) Philosophy as a way of life: spiritual exercises from socrates to Foucault. In: Arnold ID (ed.) Michael Chase (transl.). Wiley-Blackwell, Oxford

Highmore B (2010) Ordinary lives. Studies in the everyday. Routledge, London

Hillman J (2005) Politica della bellezza, In: Francesco Donfrancesco (ed.), Paola Donfrancesco (transl.). Moretti e Vitali (Bergamo)

Hillman J (2013) City and soul. In: Robert J. Leaver (ed.) The uniform edition of the writings of James Hillman, 2nd ed. Springer, Berlin

Iannilli GL (2019) L'estetico e il quotidiano. Design, Everyday Aesthetics, Esperienza. Mimesis, Milano

Kallendorf CW (ed.) (2002) Humanist educational treatises. The I Tatti Renaissance Library, Cambridge (Massachusetts)

Laertius D (1991) Lives of eminent philosophers, vol 1. Harvard University Press, Cambridge (Massachusetts)

Mortari L (2008) Conoscere se stessi per avere cura di sé. Studi Sulla Formazione. 2:45–58

Naukkarinen O (2014) Everyday aesthetic practices ethics and Tact. Aisthesis 1:23–44

Pallasmaa J (1999) Toward an architecture of humility. Harv Des Mag 7:22–25
Parsons G, Carlson A (2008) Functional beauty. Clarendon Press, Oxford
Plato (1982) Hippias Major. In: Paul Wooddruff (transl.). Basil Blackwell, Oxford
Plato (1995) Platonis Opera, In: Duke EA, Hicken WF, Nicoll WSM, Robinson DB, Strachan JCG (eds.) Tetralogiae I–II (Oxford Classical Texts), vol 1. Oxford University Press, Oxford
Pohlenz M (1933) To prepon. Ein Beitrag zur Geschichte des griechischen Geistes. *Nachrichten der Gesellschaft der Wiss. zu Göttingen.* Philolog.-Histor. Kl. 16:53–92
Saito Y (2007) Everyday aesthetics. Oxford University Press, Oxford
Saito Y (2017) Aesthetics of the familiar. Everyday life and world-making. University Press, Oxford
Saito Y (2020) Aesthetics of care. In: Zoltán Somhegyi, Max Ryynänen (eds.) Aesthetics in dialogue. Applying philosophy of art in a Global World. Peter Lang, Berlin, pp 187–202
Sartwell C (2010) Political aesthetics. Cornell Univ. Press, Ithaca and London
Shusterman R (1999) Somaesthetics: a disciplinary proposal. J Aesthet Art Critic 57:299–313
Shusterman R (2000) Somaesthetics and care of the self: the case of Foucault. Monist 83(4):530–551
Shusterman R (2012) Thinking through the body. Cambridge University Press, Cambridge
Tatarkiewicz W (1980) A history of six ideas: an essay in aesthetics. Springer, Berlin
Tedesco S (2012) Somaesthetics as a discipline between pragmatist philosophy and philosophical anthropology. Pragmatism Today 3(2):6–12
Welsch W (1997) Undoing aesthetics. Sage, London
Xenophon (1979) Memorabilia, Oeconomicus, In: Marchant EC (transl.). Harvard University Press-London, Cambridge (Massachusetts), William Heinemann
Zak G (2014) Humanism as a way of life: leon battista alberti and the legacy of petrarch. I Tatti Stud Ital Renaissance 17(2):217–240

Elisabetta Di Stefano is Associate Professor of Aesthetics at the University of Palermo (Italy). She is in the international board of *Popular Inquiry: The Journal of the Aesthetics of Kitsch, Camp and Mass Culture* and *ESPES. The Slovak Journal of Aesthetics*. Her fields of work are Everyday Aesthetics, theory of Arts in Renaissance (specially Leon Battista Alberti), theory of ornament.

Last publications*Che cos'è l'estetica quotidiana*, [What is Everyday Aesthetics] Roma: Carocci, 2017; *Designing Atmospheres. The Role of Aesthetics in the Requalification of Space*, in Mario Bisson (ed.), *Environmental Design*, DE LETTERA WP, Milano, 2017, pp. 15–21; *Cosmetic Practices: The Intersection with Aesthetics and Medicine* in *Aesthetic Experience and Somaesthetics*, ed. by Richard Shusterman, Leiden-Boston, BRILL, 2018, pp. 162–179; *The Power of the Gift. A Perspective of Political Aesthetics*, in "Popular Inquiry. The Journal of the Aesthetics of Kitsch, Camp and Mass Culture", vol. 1, 2019, pp. 26–35; *The Rhythm of Time in Everyday Aesthetics*, in Zoltán Somhegyi - Max Ryynänen (eds.), *Aesthetics in Dialogue. Applying Philosophy of Art in a Global World*, Berlin, Peter Lang, 2020, pp. 29–38.

The Body in Formation. Reflections on Body Bildung

Carsten Friberg

Abstract The author argues that the formation of the body is essential for the formation of spirit. Despite the critique is often advanced that philosophy and classical ideas neglect the body it is argued that in more forms of philosophy, the body does play a role. It is not its absence that is the problem, but rather how later readings are slack, or unwilling, in their readings to recognize it. This is unfortunate because of the importance of the bodily formation without which the formation to humanity is in danger of becoming one-sided and potentially dehumanizing.

Keywords Philosophy · Body · Formation · Halbbildung · Spirit · Humanity

Introduction

I will argue that the body is a constitutive and integrated element in formation, the term I use in English for the German *Bildung*. It may not at first appear to be the most obvious element as formation concerns a forming of spirit or mind, *Geist*, i.e. the forming of the intellectual capacity and moral character of a person of culture who is considered knowledgeable of arts and humanities. However, a person of culture should not only speak about such knowledge but also embody and act from it.

The embodiment of cultural ideals in any form is an appearance of the political, i.e. of how we organise according to norms and how we exercise powers decisive for administrating the norms. The powers appear in cultural and social matters including in the physical, i.e. bodily, presence of individuals, and the political is a distribution of powers regulating our communal living.

Appearance and embodiment should be taken literally. Embodiment is about something becoming present in a concrete physical appearance like when a gender-related difference in bodily appearance reveals an embodied practice. Iris Marion Young notices in "Throwing Like a Girl" how Erwin Straus struggles with explaining the differences in throwing between the two sexes which he believes cannot be due

---

C. Friberg (✉)
Copenhagen, Denmark
e-mail: carsten.friberg@gmail.com

© The Author(s), under exclusive license to Springer Nature Switzerland AG 2022
E. Di Stefano et al. (eds.), *Aesthetic Perspectives on Culture, Politics, and Landscape*,
UNIPA Springer Series, https://doi.org/10.1007/978-3-030-77830-9_4

to anatomy, hence must be something learned. Nevertheless, he ends with the unsatisfactory explanation that girls have a feminine style that is ultimately explained by a "feminine essence" (Young 1980: 138). Young rejects the essence as explanation. Instead, she problematizes bodily performances as acquired and adapted through upbringing and practices filled with cultural ideals and structures of power. It is exactly this point I will pursue. The gender difference is the embodiment of cultural and political structures that have influenced how we perceive and practice social relations.

I will not discuss Young's suggestion that the feminine in a Western context is due to several contradictory modalities of bodily existence (an ambiguous transcendence, an inhibited intentionality, a discontinuous unity with surroundings, Young 1980: 145 ff.). I will also not engage in empirical studies of different bodily forms of presence between social groups, towards minorities, gender etc. My focus is simply an awareness of the role of the body for the forming of an individual's presence.

My focus is philosophical, i.e. it relates to knowledge, in this case our knowledge of our presence in a social context. Regarding philosophy, it is twofold. It is the role of the body for the girl throwing something that is not merely the act of throwing but concerns the perception and self-perception of the girl; and it is the role of the body which some forms of philosophy consider as important despite philosophy's widespread reputation of being hostile towards the body.

I begin with briefly commenting on body in relation to philosophy and then address in Sect. Formation/*Bildung Bildung* to distinguish it from a curriculum tradition, liberal arts and other candidates in the field of education. A motive for taking up this topic of bodily formation is to address better the consequences of a formation only half-done, which in this case does not mean half completed but means it is a potentially dangerous failure. I touch upon this in Sects. Spiritual Sciences and Half-Education and Return to the Body where examples of a role given to the body in formation address that the forming of an intellectual capacity concerns a concrete and moral being that embodies culture, social structures, and powers.

The Body in Philosophy

I begin with the complaint often held against philosophy that it forgets the body. It does not take long to find examples that appear to confirm this view. We read, for example, in Cicero's *De re publica* that the body is a prison for the soul (e.g. VI, 14–15; fortunately, the prison is both fit and well adapted to the spirit, *De legibus* I, 26), and famous is Plato's Socrates referring to a myth that we live in a sort of prison which should be understood to be the body (*Phaedo* 62b) though we should always be careful about interpretations of Plato's dialogues taken out of context. Although prison is not a positive metaphor we should understand the body is an inescapable condition of our earthly existence though we could wish for better—what we may do when experiencing diseases, suffering, physical limitations, and ultimately death. More such examples make philosophy appear as a body hostile environment. However, philosophy is about how an appearance does not do full justice to what there really is.

I will touch upon this question by first briefly addressing an example of an ideal of rationality where the body is excluded. Such exclusion is not entirely inappropriate, but it depends on what we ask for. I ask for bodily presence in concrete human relations and that brings me, secondly, to look elsewhere for the body in philosophy.

a. The task of philosophy is to investigate forms of rationality and their claims of legitimacy whether they are made explicit or not. In more discourses today, we encounter an idea of rationality as something univocal permeating different activities. This idea can be illustrated by what Mark Johnson calls Objectivism, the idea that objective reality is mapped through concepts, being univocal and context-independent symbols and that "rational thought can be viewed as an algorithmic manipulation of such symbols" (Johnson 1987, x). Furthermore, it also "treats meaning as a relation between sentences and objective (mind-independent) reality" (Johnson 1987: 173), hence, it implies an ideal of separation of object and thinking.

Objectivism we can position in the one end of a spectre of current discussions on body and cognition (for an idea of the variety see Scheer 2012), the end neglecting or even rejecting the role of the body. Johnson opposes it by arguing for the legitimacy of embodied and imaginative structures of understanding. He calls this 'the reappearance of the body' in his book *The body in the mind*. He argues that forms of imagination "grows out of bodily experience" (Johnson 1987, xiv) as a "capacity to organize mental representations [...] into meaningful, coherent unities" (Johnson 1987: 140). This constitutes for him an essential part of a theory of meaning which must "achieve coherent, patterned, unified representations" (Johnson 1987: 168). He wishes to legitimize the inclusion of imagination into a theory of meaning and asks for a "full-blown theory of imagination" describing a set of operations on representations that can answer the Objectivist critique of a missing logic of creativity (Johnson 1987: 169). With his semantics of understanding he remains within an ideal of insisting on "meaning as a fixed relation between words and the world" (Johnson 1987: 175).

Whether he succeeds in getting recognition from the analytical philosophy he addresses is not a discussion to take here. I only use his characterisation of the Objectivist idea as illustration for a particular body hostile ideal of knowledge. Instead of discussing meaning in representations growing out of bodily experiences, I would rather change focus to discuss what *makes* representations meaningful. In this, I follow a phenomenological tradition that Johnson acknowledges has parallels to his work but he does not include in his discussions (Johnson 1987, xxxvii).

In a phenomenological approach, meaning is brought into existence *in* communication; not by associating representations and 'psychic facts' in the subject (Merleau-Ponty 1945/2002: 212 ff.). Phenomenology questions a model of knowledge that first divides subject and object and afterwards struggles with reuniting them in the subject's 'computing' of information about the object. Such a model also separates knowledge from action, assuming we first acquire knowledge then decide on an action. However, separating knowing and acting runs contrary to perception. To perceive and relate to something is the same; we are not confronted with the world but engaged in it as physical present and interacting beings (Fuchs 2000: 163 ff.; Waldenfels 2000: 82 f., 132 ff.).

The Objectivist understanding may be appropriate in, for example, a scientific approach that isolates the object through a methodological neutralisation of its environment. However, when the interest is in formation of a concrete person such ideals are inappropriate. For a concrete person, presence and interaction are essential; a person is not a mind-independent object. Obviously, the body can sometimes appear as mind-independent, for example, when we feel sick and the body will not cooperate with us. However, we must distinguish the pain we feel as a state to be in from talking about the pain in a part of our body to be examined by the physiotherapist. What we know in English as 'body' is in German either the body as object, *Körper,* like the body we know from laws in physics, or the body as our living body, *Leib*. The *Leib* is the medium in which a world appears. In this world, objects appear including my *Körper*. The difference reveals that we interpret our body; it is not something simply given, but it is something given a significance. I will not pursue this further; we find it developed in different phenomenological works of Maurice Merleau-Ponty and Hermann Schmitz for which an overview is given by Thomas Fuchs (2000: 63 ff.) and to which he himself makes an important contribution along with Bernhard Waldenfels (2000) and Gernot Böhme (2019). My point is to emphasise that our understanding of body is a matter of interpretation, and such an interpretation has political implications.

Illustrative for such implications is Jean-Paul Sartre's description of shame, of how I see others as objects and come to see myself as an object for them while also becoming aware of myself in relation to myself. He writes, "I have just made an awkward or vulgar gesture. This gesture clings to me; I neither judge it nor blame it. I simply live it. […] suddenly I raise my head. Somebody was there and has seen me. Suddenly I realize the vulgarity of my gesture, and I am ashamed" (Sartre 1943/1984: 302). What I wish to keep in mind for the following is how the example addresses a bodily appearance that reveals one's educational background: we only feel ashamed because others watch and we share the rules of behaviour with them.

b. When an Objectivist understanding that explicitly ignores the body is applied as a general idea of rationality, we can say the body is forgotten. Even though this view belongs only to specific ideals of rationality, it proves to leave an impact on more general ideas of what philosophy is like when someone with a condescending tone talks of armchair philosophy. Philosophy exercised from the armchair or the writing table becomes the target for critique from those who assume philosophy to be chained to chairs that are both positions at institutions and the work place of the sedentary philosopher "from which the real world is observed" forming the "orientation of philosophy" as Sara Ahmed quote Ann

Banfield's critique (Ahmed 2007: 152). Ahmed herself elaborates, correctly saying that what "you come into contact with is shaped by what you do" and armchair and writing table are examples of the philosopher's position that "puts certain objects within reach, just as it keeps other things in the background." We should agree with her that what "is reachable is determined precisely by orientations we have already taken" (Ahmed 2007: 152) but what I question here is how Banfield and Ahmed can assume that the philosopher's life, Ahmed's example is Edmund Husserl, is orientated from the writing table, even if some of Husserl's examples use that position. When Banfield and Ahmed use the phrase that the philosopher observes 'the real world' they subscribe to the Objectivist approach to the world.

Taking a phenomenological approach is about abandoning assumptions like 'observing the real world.' Phenomenology as a philosophical discipline asks for the origin of such ideas about world and knowledge and their possible legitimacy. Before the philosopher can sit in an armchair, some experiences with the world must have been made, and experiences include engaging bodily with it—we have never met a bodiless philosopher. The issue is not that philosophy has forgotten the body; it is to forget where to look for it in philosophy.

Odo Marquard pins the matter when he, in a hermeneutic fashion, says that "one cannot really have a philosophy without having the experiences to which it is an answer" (Marquard 1987: 8, my translation) and Merleau-Ponty writes: "I begin to understand philosophy by feeling my way into its existential manner" (Merleau-Ponty 1945/2002: 208). Philosophers would not do philosophy if they were not sentient, living beings formed by experiences and engaged in the environment—and the body is one essential component for engagement. The character of this engagement will influence who the philosopher becomes, as William James says in his lectures on *Pragmatism* in 1906, and a century before J.G. Fichte writes: "What kind of philosophy one choses depends on what kind of person one is" (Fichte 1984: 17 [SW 434/GA 195], my translation). Admitted, Fichte does not speak of the body, but it makes no sense to speak of a person without a body. The philosopher, like anyone else, is present in the world as a concrete human being living a concrete life forming the experiences that will lead to the questions asked.

Sitting in an armchair, when the philosopher comes to do that, is no less corporeal than other activities. If one holds patronizing views on armchairs, it is not for the lack of body but for judging specific practices of the body. Why should dance and performance be more bodily than walking in libraries and sitting in armchairs? The answer may be 'for the awareness of the body!' However, the performer's awareness of the body is no more of an awareness than the philosopher's, only different. The professional athlete or cyclist are making a living of their body, but they may also neglect it by pushing it beyond its limits while the philosopher may go to the gym, follow diets and remember not to sit too long in the same position and thus be attentive to the body. The question is about the kind of awareness one has when it comes to the body and that question does not privilege dancers and performers any more than art-historians and philosophers.

When arguing for the body in formation, it is the life-story forming us that we must pay attention to. An element in this life-story is practices that form our concrete acts and our perception of them. When, in the early 20th century, one went to a specific place in the house to lift one handle and swing another to ask for a connection on the phone whilst we in early 21st century can be anywhere, swiping a finger over a smooth surface to be connected to someone almost anywhere on the planet, it is not only a change in what we can do but also in how we perceive what we do. Exercising concrete tasks form perception. From cultural history we learn about such examples, e.g. how touching undergoes a change in significance. A medieval person would believe to be 'in touch with' something considered authentic and authoritative through relics, making one in touch with the holy person it comes from and in the end with God (Classen 2012: 151, see also 27 ff.). For us it has become an external relation to something, a mere symbol.

Formation/Bildung

Bildung is "the most ambiguous concept of German pedagogy, providing a range of uses and interpretations" (Alves 2019: 2). This is not the most encouraging quotation to begin with and the ambiguity matters for the choice of translation. I choose formation and ignore alternatives such as self-cultivation.

Bildung denotes a process of becoming cultivated through confrontation, alienation, and appropriation, a process that distinguishes it from education (*Erziehung*) and instruction. The end of formation is to acquire and become spirit, which here is the translation of *Geist*. Spirit is not about the psychological character of an individual but what is common and present among individuals in a community. It is what the individual aims at becoming by transcending individuality while at the same time maintaining one's individuality. Hegel can say it is "[t]he *I* that is *we* and the *we* that is *I*" (Hegel 1807/2018: 108, emphasis in original). To be at the same time individual and common sounds like a contradiction, but is only so if one does not accept the tension within determinations characterising dialectic thinking.

When formation appears in German context in second half of the 18th century it draws on both an *imago Dei* and *imitatio Christi* (Anzenbacher 1999), on an ideal or direction and an activity. Regarding activity one should keep in mind, we are in the context of German Idealism for which the active or processual character of the human subject is the foundation; where autonomy and freedom are essential characteristics for a world-constituting subject. It is the belief that man is liberated from the power of nature hitherto determining the conditions of society, liberated from the belief that society in its organization should imitate the order of nature to prevent us from unnatural living. Instead, made explicit by Hegel in Joachim Ritter's reading of him, the substance of freedom becomes positively conceptualized to form the foundation of rights and the state to provide the conditions for freedom (Ritter 1989: 23).

Such a subject is no mere tool in the machinery of the state's bureaucratic apparatus. One must ask, like J.G. Herder did, for a more organic understanding of the subject's integration by becoming human in relation to an environment in which the responsibility of the state is the formation of humanity (see Alves 2019: 5). The state needs servants, but spirit is not a servant to the state but to humanity. This idea requires a reform of the universities and academies as Wilhelm von Humbolt suggests (Humbolt 1809/10). In an age where privileges defining social roles lose their significance, such a reform appears along with the forming of new roles.

A genre of books exemplifies the process of formation, a genre known as novels of formation or coming of age (*Bildungsroman*). One is the paradigmatic novel of the genre: Goethe's *Wilhelm Meisters Lehrjahre* (*Wilhelm Meister's Apprenticeship*) from 1795/96, another to mention does not really fit in as it is not a novel but a philosophical book unfolding the building of spirit, namely Hegel's *Phänomenologie des Geistes* (*Phenomenology of Spirit*) published (1807).

In both cases, the model of formation is through moving into the world and engage with it. One leaves home, leaves the naïve relation to the world to then learn from experiences and return as a different, an experienced, person—at least if one's journey proceeds through the articulation of the experiences one makes confronted with the world. The experienced person unites in a self: what one was and what one has become. It is important to note the contrast with ideas of self-actualization. The self is not there to be actualized, but it becomes a self. It is no journey inwards to find one's true and authentic self. Ideas of an authentic self are often meant to oppose the ideals of formation by emancipating the individual from the common ideals of community. However, such an inbound journey takes an opposite direction of formation. Formation is not about the individual in its individuality but an individual related to humanity, becoming a member of society. The Hegelian 'the I that is we and the we that is I' is essential to keep in mind to maintain that the subjectivity in question is not an individual subject. The emancipation is from privileges defining individuals to become citizens, subject to the society and the principles of law and rights (Ritter 1989: 30). The purpose is to form a society based on principles protecting the individual as member of a community of equal individuals and not about an emancipation from community to define any ego as one pleases.

I do not intend to elaborate further on this tradition of formation appearing around 1800; it serves to emphasize the point mentioned with Fichte and Marquard about who one is due to how one's life has been formed by the journey one has taken in life. This journey is easily misconceived in a one-sided fashion of leaving out the concrete person to focus only on the general ideals one learns to be part of in the educated community. The one-sidedness poses a challenge: one must avoid becoming a mere follower as Theodor Adorno warns us (Adorno 1971: 97 ff.). The difficulty of leaving one's particularity to become member of a general order, of society, is to be a free subject while at the same time being subject to a common idea and order. A challenge is the imbalance of the extremes of either insisting on the individual's sovereignty or being absorbed into a community to turn over one's individuality to the common.

The difference between the experiences [*Erfahrungen*] made through the journey of learning in formation to humanity and the experiences [*Erlebnisse*] of self-actualization for one's individual desires is a difference of a journey into the world such as Goethe's Wilhelm makes it and journeys made around the world for the sake of travelling, appearing perhaps for the first time with Giovanni Francesco Gemelli Careri's *Giro Del Mondo*—the title of his 1699 book about his travels in 1693–97. His journey is for no particular purpose but his personal impulsive desire. He may be what we could call the first tourist (Sloterdijk 1999: 839), and travelling as tourist is not a matter of coming of age. Following Peter Sloterdijk, another traveller who is not on an educational journey is Phileas Fogg that Jules Verne in 1873 makes travel around the world in 80 days. It is a journey solely for the possibility of modern transportation in which events are practical obstacles and any other occurrence on the journey of no interest—no experiences are made (Sloterdijk 1999: 839 f.). Not any journey is a journey for life and for learning.

Spiritual Sciences and Half-Education

Formation, hence, is related to body by deliberately working with our concrete confrontation with the world, which cannot be merely intellectual. I wish to discuss two aspects of this. One is the awareness of the concrete body in formation, to come back to in the next section; the other is the awareness of body in our relation to this tradition of formation—a relation that is usually considered one of reading.

The role of the body in relation to the tradition of formation, and I really believe this is an example that should be applied in relation to almost any intellectual tradition, is the one of Marquard above, that to have a philosophy we need the experiences to which it is an answer. We can ask what we engage in when we read Herder, Hegel, Goethe, and Humboldt on formation. Is it to acquire a correct understanding of the texts, or is it, and this is an essential hermeneutic point, to see how the authors understand the problem of formation? It is, to come back to the girl throwing objects, a difference between describing how she throws, i.e. like a girl, and understanding what makes her behave like a girl, i.e. in accordance with an ideology constructing the role of being a girl that she, through appropriation, has made her own.

The reading of Herder, Hegel, Goethe, and Humboldt is part of a curriculum in education and could be considered a cornerstone in formation. Now, the question is whether the reading makes one a mere follower of the discussions, or if one becomes formed and embodies the humanistic ideals. Reading them belongs to the humanistic tradition of *Geisteswissenschaften*, i.e. "spiritual (or mental) sciences" (Shusterman 2012: 26). Richard Shusterman comments on the omitting of the body in these studies of the products of a free spirit that lead to appreciating spiritual achievements while bodily passive (Shusterman 2012: 37). He advocates for recognising and thinking through the body in order to cultivate ourselves (Shusterman 2012: 26), and suggests introducing bodily exercises through which students will experience how bodily exercises influence thinking processes.

Agreeing to the influence of bodily states on thinking, I nevertheless part from Shusterman's invitation to improve bodily well-being and learning skills through exercises to ask for awareness of the body as a background that forms a cognitive necessity for mental life (Shusterman 2012: 61). The challenge is not a lack of body but a lack of awareness of what is already practiced in relation to the body. A challenge is to avoid being a mere follower of an ideal of reading that keeps distance and only discusses the reading and not life. Instead, we must pay attention to how the works articulate understandings of what the good life is, coming from concrete experiences and practices. If we only read literature and philosophy as cultural products to carry out scholarly conversation about them, we take the position of Objectivism and we will find ourselves subjects to what Adorno calls *Halbbildung*, often translated half-education (Adorno 1975: 66 ff.). I return to this critique below in section c.

a. If what Fichte says about the philosopher's choice of interest depends on what kind of person one is, and if we add from Marquard that experiences are a requirement for full appreciation and understanding, we find a body as background that forms mental life. A possible misunderstanding must be prevented.

If a philosophical theory, or any other spiritual product, reflects the experience of the producer, we could ask if a requirement for appreciating Goethe is that we should share his experiences. While some shared cultural experiences are required for understanding, the consequence is not that the female reader cannot understand Goethe like the male can, or that a German understanding is privileged over a Spanish or a Nigerian. Of course, there are differences related to how the reading resonates with personal experience and knowledge, but a hermeneutic point is that despite differences we do in fact read the same text. Virgil speaks to me across time and culture even if my knowledge of his cultural environment is limited; Gilgamesh speaks as well, only gives me, because of my lack of knowledge, more interpretative difficulties. Still, they both make sense. To ask for identical life-experiences as premise for understanding is to turn interpretation into what Hans-Georg Gadamer calls a hermeneutic nihilism (Gadamer 1990: 100). One does not have to have first-hand experiences of psychoanalysis and being a woman to understand Marie Cardinale's *Les mots pour le dire* (*The Words to Say It*) though it will resonate differently to one who has. Nevertheless, I can share my reading experience with the other.

In her memoires, the Danish actress Johanne Luise Heiberg reflects on her playing Juliet in Shakespeare's *Romeo and Juliet* a second time in 1847 when she is 34; she played the role first when she was 15. While she in her first appearance was almost the age of Juliet who is 14, and she could play the role with the girl's innocent approach, she finds that the development of the character of Juliet in the play, where she matures through erotic passion, is a role that only an experienced woman and skilled artist can perform, never a young girl (Heiberg 1974: II, 162 ff.). While one's own experiences have a word in performing and reception, performing and writing can also convey to others what writer and audience have not experienced themselves—if not, how could Shakespeare write about a young woman's erotic education and an audience of different members understand it? There would be no point in arts and literature if not. Heiberg praises a reflection on acting made by Søren Kierkegaard, the contemporary philosopher living an entirely different life from her though in the same city. In *Krisen og en Krise i en Skuespillerindes Liv*, (*The Crisis and a Crisis in the Life of an Actress* (1848)) he, she writes, demonstrates a better understanding of the art of acting than many of her colleagues have (Heiberg 1973-74: II, 172 ff.). He gives words to what she, in her practice, has felt: the weight of uneasiness behind the scene and the lightness of performing when on stage which carry the nerve of performing—opposite to the rash or inexperienced actor.

It would be a misunderstanding to believe we have to share experiences with writers, whether of literature or philosophy, to understand them. However, the more they resonate with our experience the more they speak to us and affect us, i.e. our understanding becomes more than intellectual and the works prove to matter to us. My choice of the notions resonate, affect, and matter, is deliberate; they point at how the situation of interpreting is emotional and physically concrete, hence more than merely intellectual.

b. Returning to the difference in throwing objects between girls and boys, this act is one different from reading Goethe. However, the throwing is the embodiment of structures acquired through experiences and training forming the perception of what one can do. Young gives examples of female experience related to her own cultural background: "we lack an entire trust in our bodies to carry us to our aims [...] we often lack confidence that we have the capacity to do what must be done. [...] The other side of this tentativeness is, I suggest, a fear of getting hurt, which is greater in women than in men" (Young 1980: 142 f.). Our relation to other people builds on learning such physical acts, to an extent where we perform them without awareness of their origin such as the handshake which, in the Middle Ages, communicated information through physical contact better than "through the impersonal and disembodied medium of a written text" (Classen 2012: 5), obviously also serving the task better among illiterates. Such significance erodes over time, and new may arrive when, in the light of pandemics, physical contact receives attention and is occasion for a different understanding and embodied reaction.

The reading of Goethe is not where the habit of throwing stones comes about. However, through arts and literature, as well as any other form of practice, we learn how to think and act. We find discussions of this reaching back to the Greek antique concerning the audience's involvement and emotions used for the education of individuals—one can think of the second book of Plato's *Laws* where we find a detailed program for the use of music and dance for forming citizens. Arts have always been used for education to form senses, emotions, and body constituting a cognitive necessity for mental life. This is not limited to arts only, but it concerns any influence of the environment. How to throw a stone comes in the end from practices for which cultural artefacts play their role for how girls and boys behave. If Goethe has lost his position as educator, popular film can teach how one's emotional reactions should be and how one's bodily posture in specific situations should be performed—to be exercised in practice. There is no lack of body in cultural artefacts, only a lack of awareness of such existing practices and how they matter for the appearance of gendered differences, for example.

c. Neglecting the bodily practices that are present in formation is a view that comes to see formation as a one-sided enterprise while losing an essential aspect of the full formation. The negligence is of what is in fact happening, making one unable to understand why, for example, ideologies are maintained like gender differences. The neglecting view is parallel to *Halbbildung,* which does not mean formation only half done as if it was good only not good enough. *Halbbildung* makes only an illusion of being a cultivated person. It is not the first step of formation but its deadly enemy (Adorno 1975: 84).

The purpose of formation is maturity which is a purpose different from learning instrumental skills. When failing in performing the balance between becoming mature as an individual while also becoming a member of society, one only becomes a skilful actor giving the illusion of cultivation; one who is, in one and the same person, spiritual pretentious and barbaric anti-intellectual (Adorno 1975: 91). To master the curriculum of the finest cultural artefacts of the Western tradition does not also imply the acquisition of moral character. The Western culture would not have degenerated into the barbarism of the 20th century if that were the case. Formation to maturity proves to be essential (see Adorno 1971: 93).

Moral character involves the full person, mind and body. To study spirit is not like studying nature, as something there to investigate; it is to participate, it is to be oneself a spirit in the community of spirits. This poses a difficulty as any approach to spirit as an object is an approach by that same spirit which will simultaneously affect and modify the object (see Hegel 1807/2018: 56 f.). This explains why Hegel's *Phenomenology of Spirit* is not a book that begins with defining spirit and then proceeds to different characterisations, but a book about how spirit makes itself apparent when reflecting on it. Likewise, forming humanity does not follow a manual or instruction for being formed, but is necessarily a journey through life. Formation is a matter of engaging the full individual into a process of becoming a human being through a life-engaging confrontation with the world. This confrontation can be transmitted through the cultural artefacts because they resonate with our experiences and ask us to engage more directly than through expressing an eloquent criticism. In this process we need to become aware of the bodily formation at work.

Return to the Body

To conclude I will return to how appearing and embodying must be taken literally and how an example of this is what we see in the gender-related difference in bodily appearance Young discusses. This also exemplifies political structures becoming present in a concrete physical appearance something seen in half-education as an incomplete and degenerated education that is not only poor but also dangerous. Taking this notion from Adorno we should keep in mind how his reflections are guided by asking how a German nation perceiving itself as enlightened could degenerate into the barbarism of Nazism. Adorno is not known as a body-philosopher, perhaps even as hostile to the topic (e.g. Shusterman 2008: 27). However, I think we should see his critique as one directed towards idolising the body and take the opportunity to emphasize again the point that the problem is not a lack of the body in philosophy but where to look for it.

We find the half-educated person in what Kant calls the virtuoso of taste, in *Kritik der Urteilskraft* (*Critique of Judgement* (§ 33)), someone who shines in discussions of taste and culture. Lost for the virtuoso of taste is the embodied moral character. When an aesthetic judgement becomes about appreciating the artistic elements and their cultural references only, the judgement is out of touch with reality. It is culture reduced to subject only for enjoyment and entertainment. The problem is not that it does not articulate some sorts of human experiences; the question is what kind of experiences they are. This gives rise to the critique that entertainment pleases but leaves us largely detached from real concerns in life and in an affirmative relation to what should be considered as matters of concerns. Detached, because we only get a pleasant break from other concerns. Affirmative, because the experiences do not make us question or challenge these concerns and consequently make us passively accept them. The point is not that the experiences are not genuine; the one having them may be convinced they are. The problem is they are experiences of one being only a tourist through life.

This brings us back to the example of throwing like a girl where we see the importance of becoming aware of embodied habits and their ideological origins. Such habits are acquired in numerous ways, like through cultural artefacts, and they are elements in educational programs in more forms.

a. Kant addresses the question of embodied habits in his pedagogical writings. He finds it essential to impose discipline and this has to begin with children in school, hence they are sent there not only to learn something, but to become habituated in sitting still and being observant to what is present to them (Kant 1803: 5). The body must, through exercise, be controlled and formed—discipline comes before information—so the child's body becomes formed to society (Kant 1803: 20). Bodily training is of its own kind; it is not provided through laws like the moral education that concerns freedom and is directed towards maxims.

   We find more such recommendations and elaborate programmes in the age of Kant such as Johann Christoph Friedrich GutsMuth's *Gymnastik für die Jugend* (*Gymnastics for Youth*) from 1793, which is highly influenced by Rousseau's critique of how cultivation of young people is destructive to building their character. It is established that "No one doubts the great influence of the body on the mind: the physical treatment of the body, therefore, particularly in childhood and in youth, must tend to determine the character of the man" (GutsMuth 1803: 79). Consequently "for the exercise of thinking, the body is requisite to the mind. Sluggishness of body necessarily affects the intellect; and an habitual disuse of the physicial power too easily destroys the spiritual and moral" (GutsMuth 1803: 166). Disagreements are to how the training should be executed—Rousseau and GutsMuth on the one side criticise the refinement of senses that we on the other side can find many examples of in, for instance, Lord Chesterfield's letters to his son. Despite their differences they can agree to the importance of dance. Thus GutsMuth: "Dancing is an exercise strongly deserving recommendation, as it tends to unite gracefulness and regularity of motion with strength and agility" (GutsMuth 1803: 331), similar to how Chesterfield can explain to his, at this point 15 years old son, that "the greatest advantage of dancing well is, that it necessarily teaches you to present yourself, to sit, stand, and walk genteelly" (Lord Chesterfield 2008: 99, (27 September 1748)). We can add that Heiberg, who began her acting career as a dancer in the ballet, writes on the importance of plasticity for acting because there one learns to master the body and perform the best appearance (Heiberg 1973–74: I, 140 f.), obviously important on stage, but equally important for the stage of life to which Lord Chesterfield is introducing his son.

The reason for dwelling at these examples is to emphasise that body is explicitly included into education because bodily training is a training of our social skills. GutsMuth states that it is to prevent cultural degeneration and to re-educate for the sake of serenity of mind, mental beauty, and strength of understanding (GutsMuth 1803: 182). Less can 'do', focus can be on 'how', for example, the hand stretched out to greet the other person with a handshake proves not to be an instrument for performing a social relation but it is the act itself that performs that relation.

The body makes us present among people and consequently it is essential how we learn to master our physical presence. We form the body to become social and we rely on the body to get along with others through physical performance. Some of these we control such as a smile and a gesture, other are involuntary like laughing or blushing. Involuntary reactions have their origin in social behaviour we learn and appropriate to the point where they become spontaneous bodily reactions. Blushing is a social reaction that others may judge as revealing a sense of social order as in Sartre's example where we are caught doing something we feel ashamed of.

This cultivation is not an instrumental learning of how to use the body in different situations of social interaction. Of course, there is an instrumental use of the body like when we tie the shoelaces, but we also learn to be aware of the context of doing it because it is not always a neutral act. It is an instrumental choice whether one bends over or kneels; it may depend on age and flexibility.

It becomes a different matter when the choice of bending or kneeling is made by a man in jeans or a woman in a short skirt.

The problem is not that we often view our body as an object or think of it as an instrument for performing specific tasks; the problem is when this defines the relation to the body and we only see it as *Körper* and not as *Leib*. Waldenfels writes "[t]he body [*Leib*] is the visible expression of myself" (Waldenfels 2000: 210, my translation). Therefore, blushing is interesting because it reveals how body and mind meet in a reaction. We may feel we lose control and the body gives us away because it has adopted expressions of social behaviour in conflict with what we feel, and we find the body is no mere instrument for exercising different tasks; it is also an appearance of social formation we have come to embody. We learn both an instrumental use of the body and social behaviour, and the latter comes from others' reactions as well as from being affected by reading a novel, listening to music, and watching a play. We are not consumers of culture merely for pleasure and appreciation as many contemporary debates give the impression of; culture is for learning about emotional responses that harmonize with others and, through practicing the responses, become present in our behaviour.

Social norms and hierarchies become apparent in the bodily presence—the girl learns to throw a stone differently from the boy, or she learns it is not feminine to throw stones at all. The difficulty, and the possible forgetting of the body, lies in how the "formative process, *Bildung*, in the full sense, which brings about this social construction of the body only very partially takes the form of explicit and express pedagogic action" (Bourdieu 2001: 24). It is, Pierre Bourdieu can add, due to an "automatic, agentless effect of a physical and social order," something "[i]nscribed in the things of the world". A something that can be the "masculine order" which "inscribes itself in bodies through the tacit injunctions that are implied in the routines of the division of labour or of collective or private rituals" (Bourdieu 2001: 24). If the girl throws something in a different way from the boy and we assume it comes about through learning, then this gender specific difference in bodily presence and behaviour is an example of an appearance of the political. It is an embodied distribution of power. Where the body can be forgotten is when this distribution of power becomes routine to an extent that we take it to be natural, something largely done concerning differences in behaviour between genders. However, the body is subject to cultural interpretation. "It is no more natural, and no less conventional, to shout in anger or to kiss in love than to call a table 'a table'" (Merleau-Ponty 1945/2002: 220).

b. Considering the concrete body in formation should imply becoming aware of the political structures and ideologies that appear in physical training, whether it is brought about in educational contexts or simply through the influences exercised on us from other people and the physical organisation of the environment. Body formation leads to forms of bodily presence and action, like in how objects are thrown. I will advocate for the necessity of an awareness of how we find ourselves in the social environment to investigate what it is that has made, for example, the girl's presence and action when throwing like it is. What is it, present in the social environment among people and structures that form the physical act and, not least, gives it a significance that differentiate, in this case, girls from boys? It is not the task of this chapter to suggest how such a critical awareness should be developed. It is to say that when this is our concern the body is not forgotten in many, also philosophical, approaches despite the often-voiced complaint. It is also not the task to discuss the many possible approaches. Suggestions have been made, among these, obviously, the *somaesthetics* of Shusterman should be emphasized, and I will add only a few more from the phenomenolgocial tradition I have been drawing on (Fuchs 2012; 2016; Ratcliffe 2005; Slaby 2008; Slaby and Stephan 2008).

A concluding comment is to what we find in the embodied forms of norms and powers that prove decisive for forming us—what I called the political. Here appears also half-education again, and we must keep in mind its background in asking how the barbarism of the 20th century could appear in a culture perceiving itself to be cultivated. Partly, this relates to the question of individual, society and how to establish the Hegelian 'the I that is we and the we that is I' where the individual is no mere follower of the common. Mere following leads towards totalitarian. The individual must become an autonomous individual within the common (see Adorno 1971: 97). While this obviously is no simple question, I suggest the importance of including the bodily formation into the 'education to maturity' because it constitutes an important part of the formation reaching from the spiritual to letting the spiritual and moral character appear in a concrete individual capable of also executing the acts expected of the mature person.

The other person we meet is a concrete bodily person acting from the appropriated and embodied ideals of the formation. We must, as Simone Weil explains, value the sacred in a man passing by, having "long arms, blue eyes, and a mind whose thoughts I do not know" beyond the spirit to include "[t]he whole of him" (Weil 2005: 70). If we neglect the physical presence, "[i]f it were the human personality in him that was sacred to me, I could easily put out his eyes. As a blind man he would be exactly as much a human personality as before. I should not have touched the person in him at all. I should have destroyed nothing but his eyes" (Weil 2005: 71).

If we do not see a concrete physical person but only a moral constitution, we are at the verge of dehumanization. The same happens when we only to see the body. Then we arrive at what is usually thought of as perverse and inhumane, where someone is only something—as seen in objectification of the body in commercial context, in pornography or death camps. We arrive now at questions about the difficulty of body and mind related to the widespread practice of defining man as *animal rationale*. We arrive at questions whether this is a distinction that is, in fact, political and a distinction responsible for political ideals and conflicts depriving individuals of rights because they are judged to be more animals than humans, such as presented by Giorgio Agamben (2004). The body in formation thus proves to address not only the appearance of the political in examples such as the gender differentiation viewed in throwing objects, which obviously points towards any presence where a gender difference becomes the embodiment of a structure of power. It proves to address an ideal of the body of the concrete individual on which we form our understanding of humanity that in the end can be questioned.

I would like to thank Shubhangi Singh for commenting on an earlier version of the text and Rebecca Fuller for help with the language.

References

Adorno TW (1971) Erziehung zur Mündigkeit.Vorträge und Gespräche mit Helmut Becker 1959–1969. Suhrkamp, Frankfurt a.M.
Adorno TW (1975). Gesellschaftstheorie und Kulturkritik. Suhrkamp, Frankfurt a.M.
Agamben G (2004) The open. Man and animal. In: K. Attell (Transl.). Stanford University Press, Stanford
Ahmed S (2007) A phenomenology of whiteness. Feminist Theory 8(2):149–168. https://doi.org/10.1177/1464700107078139
Alves A (2019) The German Tradition of self-cultivation (*Bildung*) and its historical meaning. Educação Realidade, Porto Alegre 44/2(e83003):1–18
Anzenbacher A (1999) Bildungsbegriff und Bildungspolitik. Jahrbuch Für Christliche Sozialwissenschaften 40:12–37
Böhme G (2019) Leib: Die Natur, die wir selbst sind. Suhrkamp, Berlin
Bourdieu P (2001) Masculine Domination. In: Nice R (Transl.). Standford University Press, Standford
Chesterfield L, Stanhope PD (2008) Letters. In: Roberts D (ed.). Oxford University Press, Oxford
Classen C (2012) The deepest sense. A cultural history of touch. University of Illinois Press, Urbana
Fichte JG (1984) Versuch einer neuen Darstellung der Wissenschaftslehre 1797/98, 2nd edn. Felix Meiner, Hamburg
Fuchs T (2000) Leib, Raum, Person. Entwurf einer phänomenologischen Anthropologie. Klett-Cotta, Stuttgart
Fuchs T (2012) The phenomenology of body memory. In: Koch S, Fuchs T, Summa M, Müller C (eds) Body memory, metaphor and movement. Johns Benjamins, Amsterdam, pp 9–22
Fuchs T (2016) Intercorporeality and interaffectivity. Phenomenology and Mind 11:194–209
Gadamer H-G (1990) Wahrheit und Methode, 6th ed. J.C.B. Mohr, Tübingen
GutsMuth (1803) Youth: or a practical guide to healthful and amusing exercises: for the use of schools. In: Salzmann CG (transl.). Philadelphia
Hegel GWF (1807/2018). The Phenomenology of Spirit. In: Pinkard T (transl.). Cambridge University Press, New York
Heiberg JL (1973–74) Et liv genoplevet i erindringen I-IV. In: Wamberg NB (ed.). Gyldendal
Humbolt W (1809/10) Über die innere und äussere Organisation der höheren wissenschaftlichen Anstalten in Berlin, pp 229–241. doi:https://doi.org/10.18452/4653
Johnson M (1987) The body in the mind. The bodily basis of meaning, imagination, and reason. The University of Chicago Press, Chicago
Kant I (1803) Über Pädagogik. In: Rink DFT (ed.). Friedrich Nicolovius, Königsberg
Marquard O (1987) Abschied vom Prinzipiellen. Reclam, Stuttgart
Merleau-Ponty M (1945/2002) Phenomenology of Perception. In: Paul K (transl.). Routledge, Oxon
Ratcliffe M (2005) The feeling of being. Journal of Consciousness Studies 12(8–10):45–63
Ritter J (1989) Subjektivität. Suhrkamp, Frankfurt a.M., First edition 1974
Sartre J-P (1943/1984) Being and Nothingness. In: Barnes HE (transl.). Washington Square Press, New York

Scheer M (2012) Are emotions a kind of practice (and is that what makes them have a history)? A Bourdieuian approach to understanding emotion. History Theory 51(May):193–220

Shusterman R (2012) Thinking through the body. Cambridge University Press, Cambridge

Shusterman R (2008) Body consciousness. A philosophy of mindfulness and somaesthetics. Cambridge University Press, Cambridge

Slaby J, Stephan A (2008) Affective intentionality and self-consciousness. Consciousness and Cognition 17:506–513. https://doi.org/10.1016/j.concog.2008.03.007

Slaby J (2008) Affective intentionality and the feeling body. Phenomenology and Cognitive Sciences 7:429–444. https://doi.org/10.1007/s11097-007-9083-x

Sloterdijk P (1999) Sphären II. Globen. Suhrkamp, Frankfurt a.M.

Waldenfels B (2000) Das leibliche Selbst. Vorlesungen zur Phänomenologie des Leibes. Suhrkamp, Frankfurt a.M.

Weil S (2005) Human personality. In: An anthology. Miles S (ed.). Penguin, London, 69–98

Young IM (1980) Throwing like a girl: a phenomenology of feminine body comportment motility and spatiality. Human Studies 3:137–156

Carsten Friberg is an independent researcher. He holds a PhD. in philosophy and has been Assistant and Associate Professor at Aarhus School of Architecture and Aalborg University (Denmark). He has edited, together with Raine Vasquez *Experiencing the Everyday.* Copenhagen: NSU Press 2017 and with Rose Parekh-Gaihede *At the Intersection Between Art and Research. Practice-Based Research in the Performing Arts.* Malmö: NSU Press 2010 as well as books in Danish on Kant and the actuality of aesthetics. He has published in various journals inclduing *The Polish Journal of Aesthetics*; *Journal of Comparative Literature and Aesthetics*; *Studi di estetica*; *Popular Inquiry*; *Ambiances. International Journal of Sensory Environment, Architecture and Urban Space*; *Nordicum-Mediterraneum*; *Nordic Journal of Architectural Research* and *Artifact*.

Staged Emotions. Is a Democratic Atmospherization a Contradictio in Adjecto?

Tonino Griffero

Abstract The paper reflects upon the reason why one, when they imagine something about atmospheres in politics, normally think of the aestheticization of politics put in place by authoritarian and totalitarian regime and not of democracy: there is an attempt here, based on a neophenomenological approach to aesthetics, to sketch out the atmospheric potential (also) of democracy and propose a few points for discussing a "provisional atmospheric morality".

Keywords Atmosphere · Democracy · Atmospheric competence · Felt-bodily communication · Openness · New phenomenology

According to the neophenomenologic externalising approach adopted by my atmospherology and pathic aesthetics (Griffero 2014a, 2017a, 2019a, b, 2021), an atmospheric feeling is, at least in its exemplary shape, an example of the passive synthesis largely intersubjective and holistic that precedes analysis and influences from the outset the emotional situation of the perceiver, resisting mostly any conscious attempt at projective adaptation or epistemic correction. As an influential presence, it is inextricably linked to felt-bodily processes happening in felt-bodily isles (Griffero 2017a: 55–67, b), and is characterized by a qualitative microgranular presence (Griffero 2018a) that is, by definition, inaccessible to a naturalistic-epistemic perspective. Eluding this way any objective-reflective (and precisely for this reason inevitably just following) observation, an atmosphere is, in short and following here essentially Böhme's and especially Schmitz's perspective (Böhme 1995, 2017a, b; Schmitz 1969, 2014), more a spatial state of the world than a very private psychic state.

Now, it is well known that what I elsewhere called "atmospheric games", resulting from the different shapes of an "in-between" preceding and/or connecting subject and object, also has collective and therefore political effects. Especially if it were true that even in democracy "men never shape their conduct upon the teaching of pure reason", rather acritically giving into the impressions produced by images, words, and formulas (Le Bon 1895, XV). Nevertheless, it still seems extremely tricky to

---

T. Griffero (✉)
Rome, Italy
e-mail: t.griffero@lettere.uniroma2.it

© The Author(s), under exclusive license to Springer Nature Switzerland AG 2022
E. Di Stefano et al. (eds.), *Aesthetic Perspectives on Culture, Politics, and Landscape*, UNIPA Springer Series, https://doi.org/10.1007/978-3-030-77830-9_5

apply atmospherology to politics. The apparent elective affinity between totalitarian regimes and management of feelings, in fact, has always made it rather difficult to talk about the link between atmospheres and politics—especially democracy, of course. Yet it is precisely now, when politics often no longer communicates contents or a sense of belonging—increasingly mimetic and unthoughtful—but life styles, acting almost exactly as marketing and infotainment, that an affective approach could prove particularly useful. It already applied for those who voted by ideology, and certainly applies *a fortiori* for today's undecided opinion voter, who "is not the thoughtful 'independent' he is often pictured" (Packard 1957: 173). For this and other reasons any proposal enabling a phenomenology of atmospheres to be combined with democratic politics is worth considering.

It should also be borne in mind that in aesthetic capitalism (Böhme 2017c), show-values overshadow use- and exchange-values and convert need into desires that cannot be satisfied in principle, while free time is fully colonized by shopping and *Erlebnisse* as such: as already noted many years ago, for example, "New York restaurants now have a new thing—they don't sell their food, they sell their atmosphere". When people "go out to dinner [...] instead of 'going out to dinner' they'll just be going out to atmosphere" (Warhol 1975: 159). When, moreover, old and new media have the power to produce and control collective pathic effects more quickly and inexpensively than architecture and urban planning (Böhme 2006: 171), whether aimed at obtaining a demagogic agreement or generating an *indignados* movement, there is without doubt an ever increasing tendency to just sell atmospheres (here in the worst sense of the word) rather than well-formulated ideas.

Now we also know that, in the context of this seemingly unstoppable politics-media coalition, the contemporary global governance crisis often ends up being replaced by alarmist and sensationalist "breaking news" (Milev 2012), whose inherent emergency nature produces that anaesthetised and therefore more politically manipulable situation which one rightly could call "air design" and which, despite being the normal consequence of the artificial bond between members of any organization (Borch 2011: 33, 39–40), is today functional both to increasing consumption and to what could even be called "atmoterrorism" (Sloterdijk 2002). Despite everything a serious atmospherological thinking about politics still appears inhibited: a situation that is not exactly improved by the ambiguity of a language use that, euphemistically, defines a good political atmosphere, depending on context and expectations at all, a success or a failure to reach agreement. The academic fear of both generalising too much the notion of atmosphere as such and touching an aestheticization of politics that appears to be just a matter of political science, might in addition help to explain this gap. I believe, instead, that a pathic and atmospherological aesthetics (Griffero 2018c, 2019a), based on the externalisation or depsychologisation of affects and emotional life, would make it possible, as much as economic psychology, not only to better understand otherwise unintelligible collective phenomena such as fluctuations on the exchange, public opinion and electoral consensus—all phenomena that is difficult to trace back to conventional contractual transactions and to explain through a rationality only interested in calculating benefits and losses—but also to provide a critical atmospheric competence.

By working more closely with phenomenology and aesthetics, for example, political thinking could and should firstly investigate moods and atmospheres of public opinion, namely the climate or collective affective intentionality prevailing in a certain *milieu*, which, precisely by acting as a latent and non-thetic background, influences through a complex felt-bodily communication (Schmitz 2011: 29–53; Griffero 2017c) based on motor suggestions and synaesthetic characters the specific felt-bodily resonance tacitly leading behavioural patterns and values (even phantasmatic) of a given community. Especially by borrowing and developing Schmitz's concept of "situation" (Schmitz 2005), the political scientist-atmospherologist might ask, for example, whether the situation that is the object of criticism, or in any case of political evaluation, is (a) common or personal, (b) in place or available over a longer time frame, (c) impressive (immediately and totally significant) or segmented (manifest only in portions), (d) rooted or merely and provisionally inclusive, etc. (Grossheim et al. 2014: 53–57). Depressive megalomania or disenchanted serenity, mere legal formality or deeply involving civicness, simple geopolitical belonging or real community of destiny, reasonable hopes or self-inflicted complaints: all these and other conceivable conditions are also, indeed, real atmospheres—or at least atmospherically conditioned moods. While they force politicians to decide, more or less consciously, whether to arouse or silence them, it is sure that they can only atmospherically be studied and perhaps amended (within certain limits). Although not arbitrarily producible, contrary to what relativistic constructionism claims, a collective atmosphere can only partly be produced, in fact, through a mix of sub-atmospheric generators (which are multiple, such as climate, history, economy, architecture, communication resources, prior knowledge, etc.) (Grossheim et al. 2014: 19–24, 57–58), including expressive qualities or affordances immanent in the given situation and already settled felt-bodily habitualities, that would deserve closer examination: "collective intentionality", for example, "has to do not only with the (logical) constitutive and functional conditions of an institution called 'Supreme Court', but also with the circumstance that a Supreme Court exists and the significant fact that it looks like a temple and not like a shack" (Grossheim et al. 2014: 50–51).

First it should be stressed that, like any other atmosphere, also the political one cannot be merely considered as a transmission of signals but as a feeling poured out into a certain (pre-dimensional) space (Griffero 2014c) and for this reason responsible, in its quasi-thingly nature, for an each time specific felt-bodily communication. The first aim of a government policy but also of every executive group, for example, is obviously to suggest a syntonic emotional tone, in the worst cases even by using the so-called small talk and many baits only aiming at supporting previous assumptions: think for example of formulas, influent images, partial analogies, leading questions, factoids (Pratkanis and Aronson 2001). The manipulative expedients include, on the one hand, the rationalization of a cognitive dissonance artificially provoked in the recipient who, feeling guilty, uncritically accepts the solution offered by the source; on the other, the activation of phantasmal mechanisms by which a thing is all the more desirable the less it is (believed to be) available. Think also of the phantasmatic family which every fanaticism is based on (Bronner 2009) as well as the hasty and allegedly exemplary decisions that source and even message oblivion, pluralistic ignorance and background noise (due to too many or too few interlocutors) greatly facilitate. Exactly as in the case of packaging, which relies on a completely irrational transfer of qualities from package to content, political effectiveness, for better or for worse, counts on atmospheric feelings which could be contagious enough to prevent any probable discrepancy between the starting feeling or first impression and the following demystifying one. When on the contrary, for example, a sudden firing unmasks the optimism underlying the myth of the invisible hand or a major *gaffe* exposes the fictionality of the so-called streaming-democracy, what generally happens is that the retroactive focus on previously unnoticed inconsistencies can give life to a deep and violent "unpersuasion", which is, anyway, in turn an atmosphere, even though of cynical disenchantment now: the sad fact is that "the crowd [...] considers the fallen hero as an equal, and takes its revenge for having bowed to a superiority whose existence it no longer admits" (Le Bon 1895: 88).

Of course, being the show-value something philo- and ontogenetically embedded in human beings, it would be better to leave aside any romantic illusion of a real authentic and transparent communication and, instead, to be satisfied of making good use of appearances. One needs to admit, in fact, that show-values were also present in ideological affiliation and belonging vote, that the theatrical and spectacularized model—which can be traced back to the Baroque noble tradition of *theatrum mundi* (Früchtl and Zimmermann 2001) if not to the Augustan spectacularization (Zanker 1987)—also explains much past politics and today simply uses more widespread and iconocentric-technological tools: an everyday aestheticization that seems indeed necessary today especially because of the increasing aesthesiologically untranslatability of many global and future problems (how can indeed a politician make perceptible to the senses of their electorate, for example, the future crisis of energy resourses or an invisible and asymptomatic epidemic?) as well as of the increasingly aggressive mentality of a majority system especially based on epidermal rejection of opponents. If properly understood, however, even the actual theatricalisation–atmospherization of politics could maybe, as in the past (Münkler 2001: 152–153) soften the power and unexpectedly increase the weight of public opinion, thus showing, at most, that some political events are now nothing more than a painful and impotent attempt of politics as such to survive to much more influential and insidious power centres (international finance, media, multinational corporations, international bodies, etc.).

It should certainly be recognised that the guiding principles of liberal societies (rationalization, tolerance, egalitarianism, role of public opinion), precisely aimed at eliminating the deceitful atmospheric propaganda of absolutist politics, seem likely to weaken the power of collective emotions and atmospheres, which are the more powerful the less intentional (at the source) and conscious (in the receiver) they are. But this is exactly the reason, even in our consolidated (!?) democracies, of the actual regressive need for an auratically-atmospherically legitimated power, in other terms of a politics based again on leaderism, marketing strategies and emotive design. Yet we should try also to rehabilitate democracy from an atmospherological point of view, first of all not only valorising its rules and procedures but also discovering its emotional and sensible background again. To this end, I would like to point out, for example, the (also atmospheric) positive understatement of anyone who, without however harbouring the illusion to fully avoid any form of rhetoric, in a democratic society openly admits their uncertainties and gives precedence to a policy plan over personal and party interests. It is certainly true that procedures and compromises, typical of the democratic management as a *clasa discutidora* (according to Donoso Cortés' sarcastic judgement), generate atmospheres always less intense than the totalitarian or populistic ones. But it is necessary to learn to give value again to the specific democratic ethos, to those values that are also affects (common good, equality, recognition, individual autonomy, etc.) that might be summed up in the general concept of "openness", understood as the willingness to what is new, and which is not automatically considered as menacing only because it opens multiple and always questionable options (Ferrara 2014).

I know only too well how difficult it is that an emotional infrastructure so steeped in skepticism towards emphatic authenticity, prestige and charisma like democracy, so suspicious of the idea of being represented by superior people as to often and promptly convert the legitimating "only they" in a devastating anti-parliamentarian "why they?"—"the atmosphere of Obama is tangible: his race, his cool, his vocal cadence, the rolling, relaxed swagger of his gait, the aura of hope which swept him to the presidency, and the atmosphere of resignation which has descended on his presidency" (Grant 2013: 18)—could live side-by-side with the prestige needed by any government and authority. However, prestige and credibility, without necessarily involving fanaticism and irreversible historical process needing saviors and/or scapegoats, should also be found in democracy. According to the neophenomenological *Leib*-philosophy, whenever something (a person or a thing) gives life to a unilateral encorporation whose outcome is the partner's almost ecstatical excorporation—even if through memorable places and times, like in cultural conservatorism, or paranoid ubiquitous prevention strategies (contractual rules, insurance policies, medical instructions, political correctness, privacy protection) like in our deep alarmed welfare society—, this gives rise also in democracy to a competent and (fortunately only transitional) charismatic authority.

The solution, which is of course easier in theory than in practice, consists in resisting the emotional monopoly of charismatic atmospheres, and not only when they have clearly vanished as in the case, for example, of Leni Riefenstahl's propaganda films (*Triumph of the Will*, 1935, and *Olympia*, 1938) or, a fortiori, of Mussolini's facial expressions as he harangues the crowd from the balcony of Piazza Venezia (who still ever perceives an effective atmospheric fascination in these images and situations?). But one should also resist to the fascinating but undemocratic Far East windy model of power (that would bend the leaves without breaking them...), as suggested by François Jullien's example (Latour and Gagliardi 2006: 166–177) in the light of a model according to which, inexplicably, the wind always blows only in one direction (i.e. from power to the people). Which certainly does not mean that one should give *carte blanche* to atmospheres that otherwise risk to be so ironical to condemn people to inaction.

Roughly speaking, one should learn over and over again to appreciate even the most superficial forms of freedom, remembering the everlasting appeal of democracy to those who live in undemocratic societies and that might even be ironically summarized this way: "free countries are great, because you can actually sit in somebody else's space for a while and pretend you're a part of it. You can sit in the Plaza Hotel and you don't even have to live there. You can just sit and watch the people go by" (Warhol 1975: 146). The point is, to express in a more serious way, to appreciate the atmospheric benefit of a kind of discourse that, being in principle non-essentialist and non-cartesian, is bound to precedents and burden of proof, temporally and procedurally limited, ready only to accept what is rationally convincing (until proven otherwise), without choosing peripheral paths to elaborate messages in order to save cognitive energy. Provided that democratic ideas are not easily exportable, especially because of their inherent and even perceptual counterintuitiveness in rejecting differences and destinies, they can become genuinely efficient only when they radiate an atmosphere of openness which, also beneficially mindful of the bloody hermeneutical European civil wars over the one sole sense of the absolute sacred text (before) and of history (later) (Marquard 1981: 111 ff.), teaches us to live with uncertainty and always perfectible plausibility (i.e. not absolute truth). This atmosphere is nothing special: it is generally already perceivable, for example, in every academic meeting, which indeed, by ensuring a regular succession of talks (and opinions)—which as such deny any illusory intuition of some truthful perspective from nowhere—through this necessary deferral opens the way to a kind of "interpatience" (Peter Sloterdijk in Latour and Gagliardi 2006: 108–110) that, maybe, symbolizes the democratic *forma mentis* and atmospherization better than anything else.

It would now be the political science's turn to analyse the different kinds of democratic (collective) atmosphere, if possible without using a manifestly inadequate model such as that of the communication between an active sender and a passive receiver, but rather developing an appropriate (even if minimal) atmospheric competence (or intelligence). Only thanks to this competence one could hope to become capable of (a) staging political atmospheres (what we are not concerned with here), (b) fully feeling atmospheres, (c) understanding them (i.e. what an emotional authority, even the democratic one, necessarily consists of) and possibly (d) distancing oneself from them, that is, feeling them without being grossly manipulated by that. What has often been referred to as atmospheric "instinct" or "flair" (Tellenbach 1968: 49), here should be understood as a skill, that can also be improved through exercise: that is, the ability to critically examine the atmospheres one feels. That would enable us to benefit from a "provisional atmospheric morality" (to jokingly paraphrase Descartes).

This is not the place to delve either into atmospheric authority (Griffero 2014b), which is absolute (prototypic) when it cannot be resisted, but relative when one can resist it by appealing to a higher and critical level of personal emancipation, or into the dispute between Böhme (1995) and Schmitz (1998) about the possibility to intentionally generate atmospheres (anyway absolutely relevant as regards the issue of staging political atmospheres). We should instead say something only about the ethical consequences of this atmospherologic approach and the risk, often stressed by the opponents of the neophenomenologic point of view, of irresponsibly indulging in collective emotions. The first thing we have to say is, obviously, that what one ethically says on atmospheric authority also takes a relatively different shape depending on whether atmospheres are understood—to recall my tripartition (Griffero 2017a: 28, 49; 2018b)—as objective demonic powers—external to man, unintended, with respect to which the subjective component is reduced to the more or less critical reaction of the perceiver (prototypic atmospheres)—or as an external and objective effect but of a relationship, implicit as may be, between subject and object (derived atmospheres), or even as idiosyncratic moods, subjective and projective (spurious atmospheres).

Furthermore, being impossible to simply explain manipulation (traditionally) in terms of moral responsibility (of the manipulator) and guilty loss of self-determination (of the manipulated), because overcoming the dualism of subject/object often involves the collaboration of the manipulated in the genesis of the manipulating holistic atmospheric situation, it seems quite difficult to take a clear position about this and say what would be a not manipulated (democratic) atmosphere. It would be best, therefore, to avoid any rigid dualism between a manipulative and unethical agent and a culpably manipulated and hetero-managed receiver (Heibach 2012: 263) and to admit, on the one hand, that it is difficult to say if and when an atmosphere is not manipulated (and thus allegedly democratic), and, on the other, that bad (manipulative) atmospheres are not only the most artificial and totalitarian ones. The problem is (a) that no one is ever involved in an atmospheric appearance that one clearly sees as manipulative (such acknowledgement is only made *ex post* and often only in the third person description), (b) that a manipulative (in a non-judgmental sense: persuasive) appearance is implicit in every practice staging atmospheres, even in the most correct one, and (c) that condemning something as an illusory appearance already implies a different and phenomenologically incommensurable level of "reality", as such inaccessible to the pathic subject, for whom an atmosphere is really such as soon as it is felt by them, regardless of whether it is positive or negative, spontaneous or induced.

And yet I believe that only by acquiring a better atmospheric "competence", by no means reducible solely to the *affectus non nisi parendo vincitur*, one could really learn to appreciate democratic atmospheres, while making room for critical reflection, if this is not allowed by the authority itself (in its best practices). This is all the more true in today's globalised world, where one should be disenchanted about dangerously anonymous authorities (Schmitz 2008: 15–16)—from the "stock market" to GDP to credit SPREAD, etc. However, I think it is very important that one does not have too many illusions about (a) the perfect and rational transparency of atmospheric feelings, of which in fact we can always be aware just to a certain extent, as well as about (b) the availability of an Archimedean point less fallible than that provided by personal critical sense (Schmitz 2003: 328), given that, anyway, even the today's post-critical attitude favourable to atmospheres should not be confused with an acritical one; about (c) the generalisation of the intra-aesthetic paradigm of "suspension of disbelief", which would mean not living the atmospheric experience fully, as well as about d) the possibility to make recourse to a parameter measuring the intensity of an atmosphere, since it is absolutely uncertain whether this intensity is given by the inner peak or the manifest expression of the affect, by its duration or practical implications, and so on. In short: one will therefore have to content oneself with the previously mentioned "provisional atmospheric morality". I wish in particular to highlight its three aspects here.

(1) In order to mitigate the objection that, according to this approach, a person would be nothing but a "blind passenger of atmospheres" (Soentgen 1998: 117) one should learn how to distinguish, as far as possible—which maybe recalls, although in a secularized form, the "ability to distinguish between spirits" (1 Cor. 12,10)—between toxic (which does not mean "untrue") and benign (which does not mean "true") atmospheres, while being aware of walking on thin ice, where aesthetics and ethics mingle. It must be pointed out that toxic atmospheres, which cannot however be reduced to non-atmospheres, are not only those arousing stress and distress but also the dissuasive-sedative ones. Through them many dispositifs (in Foucault's sense) aim at defusing any social contradiction with the help both of artificial-conformist attunements (Schouten 2011[2]: 103) and of the inhibiting effects resulting from the alarmist demand, today become obsessive, to regulate every fragment of everyday experience (as Sloterdijk 1998–2004 has consistently held, especially in *Foams*).

(2) A good atmospheric competence also consists in accepting the fact that, due to the lack in our post-traditional societies of a paradigmatic place of atmospheric awareness, that is of a situation that may act as a paradigm of every other atmospheric experience, one should rather learn to have as many and different atmospheres (spatial, medial, functional, etc.) as possible—without claiming a critical position superior and/or external to them—and thus to allow the resulting experiences interact with each other. This could give rise to an affective well-being that, exactly as happens in democracy, depends on a division of powers (affective in this case) that relativizes their impact. One will learn, for example, from the most artificial atmospheres—even from the cold and procedural ones of democracy—what the peculiarities of the most natural-warm ones are, and vice versa.

(3) Lastly, a good atmospheric competence should favour and foster those atmospheres where, as happens with a *trompe l'oeil*, an early pathic-immersive step may and should be followed by an emergence phase. An atmosphere could thus be poorly manipulative when it stimulates a similar sequence. In this respect, not to mention here the case of protests offering real counter-atmospheres, an example of atmospheres that allow both immersion and emersion, i.e. are powerfully and influentially contagious without ever being oppressive and coercive, could be easily found in aesthetic experience, especially in contemporary art (Schouten 2011[2]: 106). Unlike the populist, as such hypnotic-somnambulistic, atmosphere, in fact, the critical-artistic one generates through its provocatory and irritating impact cognitive and affective discontinuities that always make a critical distance possible as well as empower whoever deeply experiences them. An atmosphere can be defined as poorly manipulative when it stimulates this sequence, when the "I" that it calls upon is neither a wholly non-reflective subject—and maybe tasteless enough to appreciate only the atmospheric character of *clichés* (such as a blue and clear sky)—nor a subject

placed at an excessive contemplative distance. Provided, of course, that such coexistence of affective-felt-bodily involvement and relatively self-reflective detachment can be demonstrated.

Surely, passiveness is neither really a problem nor a taboo for a (neo)phenomenological atmospherology whose core is precisely emotional rapture. Indeed, this approach does not give way either to an ascetic-rationalistic control of external feelings or to arbitrary projective transformations of them, but rather it allows for an always only relative distance from them. Therefore, though atmospherological insistence on emotional may bring about some risks and lead to suspect in a democratic situation, I hold it to be much less dangerous than the current guiding illusion that the emotional sphere might be universally, rationally controlled and manipulated (today even in chemical-genetic terms). As a matter of fact, the typical outcome of a rationalist-reductionist approach is astonishment and indignation about the fact that a person, despite his or her alleged proud autonomy, has not been capable of simply saying "no!" to a deeply moving collective feeling. For this and others reasons atmospheres should not be left to totalitarian regimes and demagogical strategies! My atmospherological approach especially supports the idea that an adult, even a committed democrat too, is not a person who at all costs removes the passivizing sphere and the felt-bodily influence of spatialised feelings, but rather, and more modestly, an individual who does not neurotically prescind from atmospheres but comes to terms with them in various ways, not least by trying to make a good and democratic use of them.

For a slightly different version of this text see Griffero (2019a*: 159–166).*

References

Böhme G (1995) Atmosphäre. Essays zur neuen Ästhetik. Suhrkamp, Frankfurt a. M.
Böhme G (2006) Architektur und Atmosphäre. Fink, München
Böhme G (2017a) The aesthetics of atmospheres. Routledge, London-New York
Böhme G (2017b) Atmospheric architectures. The aesthetics of felt spaces. Bloomsbury, London et alia
Böhme G (2017c) Critique of aesthetic capitalism. Mimesis International, Milan
Borch C (2011) Foamy business: on the organizational politics of atmospheres. In: Willem Schinkel and Liesbeth Noordegraaf-Eelens (ed.) Medias Res. Peter Sloterdijk's Spherological Poetics of Being. Amsterdam University Press, Amsterdam, 29–42
Bronner G (2009) La pensée extrême. Comment des hommes ordinaires deviennent des fanatiques. Denoël, Paris
Ferrara A (2014) The democratic horizon. Hyperpluralism and the renewal of political liberalism. Cambridge University Press, New York
Früchtl J, Zimmermann J. (2001) Ästhetik der Inszenierung. Dimensionen eines gesellschaftlichen, individuellen und kulturellen Phänomens. In: Früchtl J, Zimmermann J (ed.) Ästhetik der Inszenierung. Suhrkamp, Frankfurt a.M., 9–47
Griffero T (2014a) Atmospheres. Asthetics of emotional spaces. Routledge, London
Griffero T (2014b) Who's afraid of atmospheres (and of their authority)? Lebenswelt IV 1:193–213

Griffero T (2014c) Atmospheres and lived space. Studia Phaenomenol 29–51
Griffero T (2017a) Quasi-Things. The paradigm of atmospheres. Suny Press, New York
Griffero T (2017b) Felt-bodily resonances. towards a pathic aesthetics. Yearb East West Philos 2:149–164
Griffero T (2017c) Felt-bodily communication: a neophenomenological approach to embodied affects. Studi Di Estetica XLV 8:71–86
Griffero T (2018a) Come rain or come shine… The (neo)phenomenological will-to-presentness. Studi Di Estetica XLVI 11:57–73
Griffero T (2018b) Something more. Atmospheres and pathic aesthetics. In: Griffero T, Moretti G (ed.) Atmosphere/Atmospheres. Testing a new paradigm. Mimesis International, Milano, pp 75–89
Griffero T (2018c) Atmospheres and pathic aesthetics. In: Margherita Spagnuolo Lobb et alii (ed.) The Aesthetic of Otherness: Meeting at the Boundary in a Desensitized World. Istituto di Gestalt HCC Italy Publ, Siracusa, 57–74
Griffero T (2019a) Places, affordances, atmospheres: a pathic aesthetics. Routledge, London-New York
Griffero T (2019b) Is there such a thing as an "atmospheric turn"? Instead of an introduction. In: Griffero T, Tedeschini M (eds.), Atmosphere and Aesthetics. A Plural Perspective. Palgrave Macmillan, Basingstoke, pp 11–62
Griffero T (2021) The atmospheric "We". Moods and collective feelings. Mimesis International, Milan
Grossheim M, Steffen K, Henning N (2014) Kollektive Lebensgefühle. Zur Phänomenologie von Gemeinschaften. Rostocker Phænomenologische Manuskripte 20
Gustave LB (1895) The Crowd. A study of the popular mind. Dover, New York-Mineola, 2002
Heibach C (2012) Manipulative Atmosphären. Zwischen unmittelbarem Erleben und medialer Konstruktion. In: Heibach C (ed.) Atmosphären. Dimensionen eines diffusen Phänomens. Fink, München, 261–282
Latour B, Gagliardi P (eds) (2006) Les atmosphères de la politique. Dialogue pour un monde commun. Le Seuil, Paris
Marquard O (1981) Farewell to matters of principle philosophical studies. Oxford University Press, Oxford-New York, 1989
Milev Y (2012) Design governance und breaking news: das Mediendesign der permanenten Katastrophe. In: Christiane Heibach (ed.) Atmosphären. Dimensionen eines diffusen Phänomens. Fink, München, pp 285–303
Münkler H (2001) Die Theatralisierung der Politik. In: Früchtl J, Zimmermann J (eds.) Ästhetik der Inszenierung. Suhrkamp, Frankfurt a.M., 144–163
Packard V (1957) The hidden persuaders. IG Publishing, New York, 2007
Pratkanis AR, Aronson E (2001) Age of propaganda: the everyday use and abuse of persuasion. Freeman, New York
Schmitz H (1969) System der Philosophie. III.2 Der Gefühlsraum. Bouvier, Bonn
Schmitz H (1998) Situationen und Atmosphären. Zur Ästhetik und Ontologie bei Gernot Böhme. In: Michael Hauskeller et alii (ed.) Naturerkenntnis und Natursein. Für Gernot Böhme. Suhrkamp, Frankfurt a.M., pp 176–190
Schmitz H (2003) Was ist Neue Phänomenologie? Koch, Rostock
Schmitz H (2005) Situationen und Konstellationen. Wider die Ideologie totaler Vernetzung. Alber, Freiburg/München
Schmitz H (2008) Die Legitimierbarkeit von Macht. In: Hasse J, Kluck S (ed.) Zur Legitimierbarkeit von Macht. Alber, Freiburg/München, 5–19
Schmitz H (2011) Der Leib. De Gruyter, Berlin/Boston
Schmitz H (2014) Atmosphären. Alber, Freiburg/München
Schouten S (2011)[2] Sinnliches Spüren. Wahrnehmung und Erzeugung von Atmosphären im Theater. Theater der Zeit, Berlin
Sloterdijk P (1998–2004) Spheres, vol 3. Semiotext(e), Los Angeles, 2011–2016

Sloterdijk P (2002) Terror from the air. Semiotext(e), Los Angeles 2012
Soentgen J (1998) Die verdeckte Wirklichkeit. Einführung in die Neue Phänomenologie von Hermann Schmitz. Bouvier, Bonn
Tellenbach H (1968) Geschmack und Atmosphäre. Müller, Salzburg
Warhol A (1975) The philosophy of Andy Warhol (from A to B and back again). Harcourt Brace Jovanovich, New York and London
Zanker P (1987) The power of images in the age of Augustus. University of Michigan Press, Ann Arbor

Tonino Griffero is Full Professor of Aesthetics (University of Rome "Tor Vergata", Italy), editor of the book series "Atmospheric Spaces" (Mimesis International), "Sensibilia" (Mimesis-Studi di estetica) and the e-journal "Lebenswelt". Recent books*Atmospheres. Aesthetics of Emotional Spaces*, Routledge, London-New York 2014; *Il pensiero dei sensi. Atmosfere ed estetica patica*Guerini, Milano 2016; *Quasi-Things. The Paradigm of Atmospheres* Suny, Albany (N.Y.) 2017; *Places, Affordances, Atmospheres. A Pathic Aesthetics*, Routledge, London-New York 2019, *The Atmospheric "We". Moods and Collective Feelings*, Mimesis International, Milan 2021. Co-editor *of Psychopathology and Atmospheres. Neither Inside nor Outside*, Cambridge Scholar, Newcastle upon Tyne 2019 and *Atmosphere and Aesthetics. A Plural Perspective*, Palgrave Mac Millan, Basingstoke 2019.

Neutral Arts to Democratic Values. The Case of Iranian Naghashi-Khat (Calligram)

Majid Heidary

> I like Carl Andre's statement that "life is the link between art and politics. (Lippard 1984)

Abstract The paper highlights how some arts may promote social and democratic values while others promote non-democratic tenets. Besides, there are a great number of arts that remain silent or neutral to any social and democratic principles. The literature on the relationship between democracy and art is mostly about the possible contributions of arts to democratic values, ignoring huge number of neutral arts mostly produced in non-democratic societies. Naghshi-khat (Iranian Calligram) is a good example of neutral arts to democracy. Being formal, abstract and decorative, this artistic genre replaces the seemingly valid picture of the governments' ideology with the lived experience of people through national symbolism and poetic appearance. It enjoys governmental support and good sales in the art market mainly at the expense of remaining ignorant to the oppression imposed by the government. Neutral arts dismiss any figure, content or signifier that can refer to political or social elements, disarming any meta-analysis. Such arts escape to abstraction, poetic, decorative and symbolic appearance to avoid any friction with harsh reality of society including censorship and repression.

Keywords Neutral arts · Democratic values · Iran · Nahjashi-khat · Calligram · Hijab

Introduction

A figureless painting can be interpreted as an artist's authentic search for new forms and meanings and it is quite acceptable. On the contrary, in a society (such as Iran) where naked figures are not allowed to be presented in galleries as the state insists on Hijab and does not welcome much diversity in people's clothes, figurative paintings can be very challenging. In other words, the artist should find artistic solutions by

M. Heidary (✉)
Mashhad, Iran
e-mail: m.heidari@ferdowsmashhad.ac.ir

© The Author(s), under exclusive license to Springer Nature Switzerland AG 2022
E. Di Stefano et al. (eds.), *Aesthetic Perspectives on Culture, Politics, and Landscape*,
UNIPA Springer Series, https://doi.org/10.1007/978-3-030-77830-9_6

which naked bodies and women in erotic poses are not portrayed, and clothes conform to the norms of the society. Clearly, one of the easiest solutions would be resorting to nonfigurative painting. What I attempt to confer is that nonfigurative art can offer different interpretations based on the conditions under which they are produced. Under democratic and nondemocratic conditions, the same artistic genre can convey different meanings, only if we take the social and political conditions surrounding the artwork production into account. However, as in the above example of nonfigurative paintings, all paintings presented on the walls of galleries or webpages seem to be the same in terms of genre.

There are many aspects regarding art and aesthetics; yet when it comes to arts produced under systematic oppression, we might be able to claim that art and artistic works have a direct relation to free will. In such conditions, it is supposed that art is a process that starts with an artist and their free will and continues with viewers who also have free will in their interpretations and understanding. Any intervention (by states or institutes) in this process can alter the meaning of art from a creative *act* of free will to an economic or ideologic *react*. By creative act of free will, I am referring to an art that comes to existence from lived experiences of an artist under democratic conditions, when the artist or creator enjoys enough freedom to express their own individual story or the society they live in. Under democratic conditions, art is free to represent the real world, celebrate possible worlds, promote democratic conditions, protest against values it dislikes, or even keep silence toward any social or political values. And by economic and ideologic react, I am pointing out arts that come to existence out of constraints imposed by states or any institutes. In nondemocratic conditions, there are often constraints against creative expressions throughout the entire process: from the creation of art by the artists to the possible interpretations of the viewers. In such conditions, art mainly limits itself to functions such as protesting the status quo or the ideologic set of beliefs, celebrating the nostalgia, or keeping silence out of fear of censorship.

As for the relation between arts and politics, we can focus either on the artist's take on the role of her/his art in social changes or on the tangible contribution of their art regardless of artists' views. In the former case, we are referring to what artists think of major political and social changes and how they express their positions in artistic expressions; and in the latter case, as Steyerl (2010) claims, instead of looking at how art represent political issues, we can look at what it actually does and not what it shows. This is a pragmatic approach that emphasizes the real function of art in any given society rather than the artist's statements; meanwhile, artists may have different positions toward collectivism or individualism, or they may understand different functions for art. However, in the end, it is the realization of freedom of speech in a given society that shapes the arts and their functions.

In fact, we can claim that the relationship between arts and politics involves two aspects: appearance of the arts (or what the arts show) and function (or what the arts do). Here, we would like to examine the possible functions of an exemplary art (Iranian Calligram) in a given society (Iran). It is understood that art as an activity or engagement can contribute to social and political changes and democratic values; however, there are many varieties of arts that appear to be neutral to any social changes and remain silent towards democratic values. Neutral arts are mainly produced in non-democratic societies where there is no tolerance to any authentic search for meaning and all metaphors should conform to the dominant ones.

We normally ask about the possible contributions of arts to democracy and political changes because we believe that art is a kind of holy activity carried out by genuine artists (Schaeffer 2009). Nevertheless, through a practical lens, we would be able to ask about the benefits of this activity for the society. The majority of literature (as we will review in the following) on the relation between arts and democracy are about the possible contributions of arts to social and political changes while many varieties of arts that not only stay neutral to democratic values but also align with conservative beliefs are overlooked.

Review of Literature

It is supposed that the artists' apathy towards social changes (under nondemocratic conditions) is mainly derived from lack of proper education and critical thinking on one hand, and espionage or surveillance of the government on the other. Dewey has a very clear understanding of this situation: "When I think of the conditions under which men and women are living in many foreign countries today, fear of espionage, with danger hanging over the meeting of friends for friendly conversation in private gatherings, I am inclined to believe that the heart and final guarantee of democracy is in free gatherings of neighbors on the street corner to discuss back and forth what is read in uncensored news of the day, and in gatherings of friends in the living rooms of houses and apartments to converse freely with one another" (Dewey 1976).

However, Dewey's rendition of democracy still remains a far-fetched dream for many countries. Democracy has become a prevalent discourse in many parts of the world. Nevertheless, it is devoid of any potential implications and is mostly used by authoritarian states hiding under its guise; it is only a minimalist and formal type. The process of democratization, especially in the Third World, is considerably uneven in terms of consolidation and stability (Qadir et al. 1993).

John Dewey finds life a self-renewal process. The notion of renewal is related to communication which is "a process of sharing experience till it becomes a common possession" (Dewey 2001). As we live in society, we need certain institutes to organize this communication or experience-sharing process. It is the duty of social environment or society to envisage ideals for our behavior and communications and engage us in activities or educational programs to reach those ideals. Throughout this process, we should keep in mind that education cannot be done via direct teaching, but through intermediacy of environment. Aside from different meanings of education such as growth, preparation, unfolding, training of faculties, formation of mind, and reconstruction, Dewey finds the concept of *democracy in the heart of education.* In his perspective, there are two traits that characterize any democratic society: recognitions of common interests and continuous readjustments to new situations (Ibid).

Likewise, citizens of nondemocratic societies are usually deprived of the chance to see the world through different lenses and they lack the empathetic view. This suggests that they lack the kind of contingency Richard Rorty expects citizens to have: "...the citizens of my liberal utopia would be people who had a sense of the contingency of their language of moral deliberation, the characteristic genre of democracy, and thus of their consciences, and thus of their community. They would be liberal ironists... people who combined commitment with a sense of the contingency of their own commitments" (Rorty 1989).

With regard to the relationship between art and democracy, the bulk of related literature have focused on the contribution of art to democratic values. Raeber (2013) finds art a crucial resource for democratic citizenship and for the process of democratic deliberation. He mainly focuses on Rorty's idea that novels are the characteristic genre of democracy and they help people to develop and stabilize capabilities that are ideal for any democratic society, i.e. anti-foundationalism and a disposition for solidarity.

Another research was carried out to explore opportunities for democratic action and learning in a number of artist-led gallery education projects in the South West of England. The researchers also did their best to indirectly teach young people a certain degree of democratic activism (Lawy et al. 2010).

The main questions raised in a book titled, "Doing Democracy, Activist Art Cultural Politics" are about the ways through which art and cultural forms can help democracy and the ways by which art can move the society toward political activism; moreover, these inquiries discuss how art can use the capabilities of individuals and groups to influence the world in positive and constructive ways and the role art plays for the marginalized groups of the society (Love and Mattern 2013).

Vali and Hollands used John Dewey's 'creative democracy' to carry out a number of democratic activities in art institutes which can help creativity in everyday life. The practiced activities in this institute included placing artistic outputs under collective scrutiny and presenting them to collective brainstorming of ideas for arts. Such extended participation proved to help group trust and solidarity (Vail and Hollands 2013). They concluded that "democracy produced significant benefits both for individual artists and for the group as a whole: by subjecting their artistic outputs to collective scrutiny, they exposed their creative ideas to diverse points of view so as to enhance the overall quality of their work; joint participation in these democratic processes heightened the legitimacy of their creative outputs and solidified their collective identity; and extending participation helped improve group trust and solidarity" (Ibid).

Therefore, the contribution of the imaginary and creative world of art to democracy is significant in a number of ways. Art can extend participation in social changes, arouse a sense of belonging to a democratic and rational society, enable coexistence among diverse points of view and dispositions for democratic citizenship and solidarity, and finally, help us to adopt anti-foundationalism.

Ultimately, it is true to acknowledge the contribution of art to democracy, mostly in democratic societies. However, the concept of art is different in many aspects in authoritarian countries where arts significantly lose their social functions and become decorative, symbolic, romantic, and nostalgic elements of life. Such arts are neutral to democratic values and social changes; nontheless, there exists a certain, limited, and repressed use of art that protests. One of the classic stories of art as a weapon is the story of Fela Kuti, Nigerian composer and political activist (refer to LeVine 2015).

Given the fact that the state in nondemocratic societies supports only one ideology and its devotees, many groups of people and their voices are systematically oppressed. Under such conditions, artists and arts can be the voices of these oppressed groups. Such arts, with any form or style, attempt to protest against religious, ideological, and prejudiced beliefs rather than contribute to democratic values.

In other words, we can say that under ideal (democratic) conditions, artists enjoy freedom of expression as well as the liberty in what to show in art and what to do with art. In such cases, art is an authentic act of meaning searching, and meaning making. Arts find new metaphors and explore new possible worlds. On the other hand, in nondemocratic societies, artists are oppressed and their choices are limited to the safe ones. In these situations, art may adopt a *reactive nature* against the oppression or remain *neutral* to any social and political changes.

Iranian Naghashi-Khat and Democratic Values

The case of Iranian calligraphy-painting (calligram or Naghashi-khat) exemplifies several important features of the contemporary Iranian society as well as neutral arts to democratic values. In other words, it is a genre of art that remains silent towards social and political issues.

During the last millenium, Arabic and Persian languages have nearly shared the same alphabet and religion (for the majority of population). As Quran is written in Arabic, calligraphy is known to be a sacred type of art that is directly related to the holy scripture. Furthermore, calligraphy is supposed to have a holy origin in Islam and has played a key role in Islamic art and architecture.

Since the prophet of Islam's miracle is believed to be the Quran, the main form of Islamic art is calligraphy that is the art of writing and recording the Words of God in beautiful and artistic ways. "The primordial creative act was at once the Primordial Word which is the origin of all sounds and of the Noble Quran as a sonoral universe, and the primal point which is the origin of the sacred calligraphy that is the visual embodiment of the Sacred Word" (Nasr 1987).

The Quran was originally and mostly oral revelations which were later recorded in a written form that is now known as the holy book of Quran. "It seems very likely, therefore, that upon Muhammad's death, sections of the revelations had been memorized by heart, and other segments were preserved in a written form" (Dammen McAuliffe 2007).

Therefore, calligraphy has always played the main role in keeping the Quran safe from any manipulations. It is also worth stating that as soon as the Quran was written, other issues such as translation, decorative arts, publishing, and binding were inevitable.

Aside from the holy origin of calligraphy and its religious functions, it is also deeply interwoven with the Persian literature, Persian painting, and the art of book making. The most important Persian classic works of literature such as the Shahnameh and certain books of Saadi and Nezami were made into rather precious books that boast outstanding paintings and calligraphy. There has always been a great interdependency between calligraphy and painting in Iranian arts. Painting and calligraphy existed hand in hand in different books as well. However, this dependency had its ups and downs; at the beginning, they were inseparable. Then, they were separated and finally rejoined in a quite modern style within the contemporary art.

"In the final decades of the 14th and the initial decades of the 15th century, there was an overall decline in the width-to-height proportion of manuscript pages resulting in a narrower, taller format. As the written surface was narrowing, painting also began occupying a greater proportion of the page's total area. Thus, compositions which often involved a horizontal format and occupied no more than one-third of the height of a page in the 14th-century Shahnameh manuscripts would often be transformed into vertically oriented scenes occupying one-half to two-third of the space reserved for the text in 15th-century copies" (Hillenbrand 2000).

Initially, Persian miniatures were an inseparable part of a big art, i.e. book making. A group of artists used to get together under the supervision of a patron (usually a king or a member of royal family), to do the designing, writing (calligraphy), bookbinding, and decorating a literary text. Gradually, from Safavid era (1501–1736) to Ghajar (1789–1925), painting took its own path and tried to become an independent art in which kings and the royal court were mostly portrayed. In Pahlavi era (1925–1979), painting became even more independent from the state and found its global-like fine art functions. However, near the end of this era, painting and calligraphy joined each other once again in a modern style of Naghashi-khat (calligram).

Iranian artists of the 1960s started to bridge the gap between traditions and modern art using Iranian traditional forms, patterns, and symbols as the main elements in their arts. This movement was later called Sagha-khane style. Saghkhane means a small room in public passage ways where local people could drink water from small bowls chained to a big bowl. Later, they became religious places where people could light candles and hold religious pictures and elements. The idea of Naghashi-khat (coined in Persian through joining the two words, "*naghashi*" and "*khat*", respectively meaning painting and line in calligraphy) which involved using calligraphy in painting, was born from this artistic movement. Prior to the Sagha-khane movement, there used to be an entertaining use of calligraphy; yet in 1960s, this kind of decorative and artistic use of calligraphy became quite common. As a matter of fact, the type of Naghashi-khat that became prevalent in Iran and later in many other Arabic countries is quite different from the idea of Calligram in the English script. Naghashi-khat is a kind of abstract thinking about the idea of calligraphy. This style of calligraphy freed itself from the rules and boundaries of traditional calligraphy and made a great attempt to progress toward modernism. Naghashi-khat was a rather new and audacious step in the longstanding tradition of calligraphy and had its roots in the holy concepts of Islam (Ouji et al. 2009).

In summary, Naghashi-khat might be considered a step forward in contemporary evolution of the art of calligraphy: an abstract, energetic, and artistic reinterpretation of traditions of calligraphy. The story behind the prevalence of Naghashi-khat in Iran is an interesting one. It appears that this artistic style became popular in Iran during two quite different periods that enjoyed the support of two ideologically different governments. The first period was before 1979, when it was supported by Farah Pahlavi, Shah's wife, with focus on the Iranian national identity in the face of global art; the second period was in the 2000s, by the Islamic Republic to celebrate the Islamic face of Iranian art (Ardakani et al. 2016).

The reasons behind the supporting of Naghashi-khat by governments with quite different ideological backgrounds (the former with a national ideology and the latter religious one) shows that such arts have specific characteristics that make them appropriate for representing governmental (or institutional) artistic tastes. Iran has always suffered from lack of democracy and a democratic government in its history, specifically in its modern era, from Safavid era to Qajar, and from Pahlavi period to the Islamic Republic. The last two, i.e. Pahlavi and Islamic Republic, had severe issues with their democratic status and stability. Therefore, there is a clear relationship between nondemocratic conditions in the last 6 decades (1960–2010s) and the status of art, specifically neutral arts to democratic values; and Naghishi-khat is a bold example of this situation.

We can claim that Naghshi-khat is neutral to democratic values due to its three outstanding features: being formal, abstract, and decorative. Naghashi-khat was started with a number of modern artists who were traditionalists at heart and has maintained its popularity as a result of being potentially formal, decorative, and abstract.

During the 2000s, this art became very dominant considering the fact that it was able to present the Islamic-Iranian picture to the world and there was a high demand in Arabic Art markets for it. Besides, Naghashi-khat was in harmony with the new generation of theorists called the 'Traditionalists School' (Ibid).

The Traditionalist School had a significant influence on contemporary artists, art, and its interpretation (Heidari 2016). Traditionalist thinkers like Rene Guenon, Ananda Coomaraswaky and Frithjof Schuon generally believe in the demise of traditional forms of knowledge within the Western culture and instead they believe in perennial wisdom or perennial philosophy. They have tried to present new, flexible, and modern interpretations of Islam and its heritage so as to place it in a better dialogue with values in the contemporary world.

One of the most important features of neutral arts to democratic values is that such works are purely formal. Being formal involves *dismissal of any figures, contents or signifiers that may refer to any political, social, national, or historical element.*

"The history of Naghashi-khat merely shows the formal evolution of such arts and we cannot place them under any kind of semiotic analyses in order to reach an image of the society, cultural conditions, social events, or specific conditions of the society" (Ardakani et al. 2016).

Nondemocratic conditions support and encourage such arts and art movements due to the fact that not only are they non-threatening to conservative and nondemocratic beliefs, but also encourage conservatism in a very modern and artistic fashion. Formal arts represent the values and norms of the conservative approach or probably, foundationalism of the society, in an artistic and modern manner; however, art's medium and its subjective expression appear to belong to democratic societies.

Formalism might be taken into account as a very modern approach in democratic societies, while in nondemocratic countries, it is regarded as a sideway that has the exact opposite function. Formal arts remove social, political, or historical signifiers of arts to turn them into unthreatening, idle, and inherently nonsocial works while encouraging the current traditions and norms of the society.

The same is true for the second and third features of neutral arts to democratic values. Similar to Naghashi-khat that is abstract and decorative, most neutral arts lack any social functions as well, while they portray national or religious symbolic and abstract elements. In nondemocratic societies, abstraction is a very contemporary and artistic fashion adopted to escape from social functions of art and censorship. Abstract and decorative arts enjoy tacit agreements with states; governments can easily confiscate such arts for their nondemocratic purposes, artists can escape censorship, and finally, both democratic and nondemocratic art markets welcome them; as Naghshi-khat sells well in the art market.

Arabic countries are known as one of the most important potential buyers of Naghashi-khat works (Ibid). And even the democratic societies consider such works to be decorative that represent the original and historical backgrounds of oriental countries.

The case of Naghashi-khat is a very bold example of what usually becomes of arts under nondemocratic conditions; in fact, in all art mediums, neutral, formal, abstract, decorative, and poetic styles are encouraged by governments. What is meant by 'poetic' is a detached view from praxis and activism that changes the reality in one's mind to make it more tolerable.

"Iranian filmmakers have utilized the open image to circumvent a particularly strict form of censorship and point to the plurality of truth and experience in a political context where a repressive notion of one truth is imposed by the state" (Chaudhuri and Finn 2003). This cinema was accomplished by Iranian directors such as Kiarostami, Makhmalbaf, and many others who did their best to keep their arts away from any direct reference to political and social facts, similar to what happened to Naghashi-khat. Most of Kiarostami's movies take place in remote villages where there is minimum contact with the contemporary Iranian social norms; however, "the appeal of New Iranian Cinema in the West may have less to do with 'sympathy' for an exoticized 'other' under conditions of repression than with self-recognition. The open images of Iranian film remind us of the loss of such images in most contemporary cinema" (Ibid).

Stories written in the last decades whose characters leave the country, as well as those in which the setting is outside Iran are both referred to 'immigration literature'. The same line of interpretation is true for such arts. In other words, writers escape from nondemocratic conditions of the real society and search for meaning and identity in places where searching is safe and without consequences. Likewise, the governments' urge to produce 'global arts', a discourse being buttressed by the state, implies that the state supports arts and artists who make their works formal and abstract, free from national and political references, and paint a happy, modern, and ideological picture of the country, which is in stark contrast with reality.

Conclusion

Democracy and democratic conditions play a defining role in shaping the appearance and functions of arts. If we focus on the functions of arts in society, we find that arts are free to portray or celebrate any possible worlds under democratic conditions; we can also find the authentic *acting role*. In such cases, the artist deforms or deviates from the real world in a dramatic way that appears to be a kind of discovery of new forms and meanings. However, under nondemocratic conditions, arts assume very limited functions such as protesting the status quo or staying neutral to social and political changes; hence the *reacting nature*. In fact, arts feel numb to social and political changes and prefer to remain silent and stay neutral to the society, mainly due to the possible hazardous consequences.

In nondemocratic societies, diversity is not welcome and people are to conform to the norms imposed by states; subsequently, passiveness and neutrality among people would become prevalent. Many artists share the same passiveness and neutrality in their arts. They are not inclined to act authentically or independently in order to make social and political changes; however, art is still regarded as an activity for the elite members of the society with metaphysical origins (refer to Schaeffer 2009). Concerning artists conformity with other members of the society and becoming passive to social and political changes, we can refer to Ricoeur's claim that people find themselves "as" others: we cannot find or think about ourselves without others. This is so strong that I find 'myself inasmuch as being other' not similar to others. (Ricoeur 1992).

Neutral arts to democratic values can be found in any democratic or nondemocratic society. In the first case, neutral arts show the artist's *unwillingness* to participate in free democratic societies; yet in nondemocratic societies, they display the (un)intentional *escape* from oppression and censorship of the state.

It is wrong to assume that Naghashi-khat is representative of the contemporary Iranian art since this artistic movement is the result of nondemocratic conditions of the society under which many other art forms, media, and styles are oppressed. Naghishi-khat and other formal, abstract, and decorative arts mainly represent the taste, conceptions, beliefs, and ideological inclinations of the state rather than people. Such art, aside from its aesthetic values, (un)intentionally misrepresents the current society and replaces the picture of the state with that of the people.

In addition to misrepresenting the current society, Naghashi-khat never actively engages people in social and political activism and fails to influence the society in positive and constructive ways. Moreover, it could never be the voice of those who were oppressed or ignored. Instead, Naghashi-khat confirms and justifies power relations and the dominance of longstanding conservative traditions.

Contemporary Naghashi-khat enjoys attractive visual forms and energetic movements; it also occupies a good share of the art market. Aesthetic values of this art style and its development, however, are always in accordance with the doctorines of nondemocratic states.

References

Ali Mohammadi Ardakani, Javad Pajoheshfar, Parnia (2016) The analysis of the representation of traditionalist's approach in the Naghashi-khats done in 2000s. Negareh 35
Chaudhuri S, Finn H (2003) The open image: poetic realism and the New Iranian Realism. Screen 44(1):38–57
Dammen McAuliffe J (ed.) (2007). The Cambridge Companion to QURAN
Dewey J (1976) Creative democracy: The task before us. In: Boydston J. (ed.) John Dewey: The later works, 1925–1953, vol. 14, pp. 224–230. Carbondale: Southern Illinois University Press (Original work published 1939)
Dewey J (2001) Democracy and Communication. The Pennsylvania State University
Heidari M (2016) The Plights of Aesthetics in Iran. Contemporary Aesthetics, vol. 14
Hillenbrand Robert (ed.) (2000) Persian Painting: from the Mongols to the Qajars: studies in honour of Basil W. Robinson. I. B., London and New York
Lawy R, Biesta G, McDonnel J, Lawy H, Reeves H (2010) The Art Democracy: young people's democratic learning in gallery contexts. Br Edu Res J 36(3):351–365
LeVine M (2015) When art is the weapon: culture and resistance confronting violence in the post-uprisings Arab World. Religions 6 1277–1313. www.mdpi.com/journal/religions
Lippard LR (1984) Get the message? A decade of art for social change, 1st ed. Ep Dutton, New York
Love NS, Mattern M (eds) (2013) Doing democracy, activist art cultural politics. State University of New York Press
Nasr SH (1987) Islamic art and spirituality. State University of New York Press
Ouji M, Zindashti SZ (2009) Ketabe Mahe Honar, Naghashi-khati; a young and original in Iranian Contemporary Art. Ketabe Mahe Honar 135:30–37
Qadir S, Clapham C, Gills B (1993) Sustainable democracy: formalism vs substance. Third World Quarterly 14(3): 415–422. http://www.tandfonline.com/loi/ctwq20
Raeber MI (2013) The art of democracy—Art as a tool for developing democratic citizenship and stimulating public debate: A Rortyan-Deweyan Account. Humanities
Ricoeur P (1992) In: Blamey K (transl.) Oneself as Another. The University of Chicago Press
Rorty R (1989) Contingency, Irony and Solidarity. Cambridge University Press
Schaeffer JM (2009) In: Rendall S (transl.) Art of the modern age, philosophy of art from Kant to Heidegger. Princeton University Press
Steyerl H (2010) Politics of art: contemporary art and the transition to post-democracy. E-flux J 21
Vail J, Hollands R (2013) Creative democracy and the arts: the participatory democracy of the amber collective. Cult Sociol 7(3): 352–367. sagepub.co.uk/journalsPermissions.nav

Majid Heidary is Assistant Professor and Head of Visual Communication Department at Ferdows Institute of Higher Education, Mashhad, Iran. He is a PhD in Aesthetics and has series of papers on Iran's art, narrative and metaphoric expression. He also designs and practices some participatory art projects, and records philosophy podcast in Farsi called Praxis. Pubblications*The Plight of Aesthics in Iran*, "Contemporary Aesthetics", 2014; *The Meaning of "Artistic Creation" for Kant and Heidegger and its Comparison with Ricoeur's Understanding of "Narration"*, Kimiya-ye-Honar, 2017; *The Role of BADI (Persian Rhetoric) in Iran's Aesthetics*, "The Journal of Cognition", 2019; *The Methodology of Iranian-Islamic Aesthetics with Focus on the Relation between Mysticism and Scholastic Theology*, "Research in Art and Human Sciences", 2020.

Landscape Aesthetics and Politics

Mateusz Salwa

Abstract The aim of the article is to show that the landscape conceived of as an aesthetic 'object' has a conspicuous political significance. Contrary to what still seems to be the dominant approach, landscape aesthetics should not treat landscapes mainly as sources of aesthetic pleasures quite similar to the ones offered by painted *paysages*. A much more theoretically and practically promising perspective is achieved when the concept of aesthetics is understood in line with the original meaning of the term, i.e. as denoting sensory experience. Consequently, landscapes turn out to be aesthetic insofar as they are sensory environments. As such, they are political at their core, as any such environment is shaped by politics, and likewise for the sensory (aesthetic) experiences they offer. Hence, landscapes may be defined as sensory appearances of the political. It, then, seems advisable that landscape aesthetics should play a conspicuous role in landscape theory dominated by sociological, economic and cultural approaches.

Keywords Aesthetics · Environment · Landscape · Politics · Rights · Sensory experience

Introduction—The Political Significance of Landscapes

Landscape is, beyond any doubt, a 'travelling concept' (Bal 2002) whose manifold meaning is a result of its long itinerary that has led through various cultural fields over the centuries (Olwig 2019)—politics and art, to name just two of them—as well as a number of scientific disciplines such as anthropology, archaeology, art history, cultural studies, geography, law etc. (Antrop 2013; Kühne 2018a, b). As a result, today's meaning of the term 'landscape' cannot be univocally defined, at least not in the humanities, since it covers all of the interpretations offered by all the fields and disciplines it met during its lifetime. Hence, it is generally agreed that the concept of landscape—as well as practical issues concerning it, e.g. landscape

---

M. Salwa (✉)
Warszawa, Poland
e-mail: mateusz.salwa@uw.edu.pl

© The Author(s), under exclusive license to Springer Nature Switzerland AG 2022
E. Di Stefano et al. (eds.), *Aesthetic Perspectives on Culture, Politics, and Landscape*,
UNIPA Springer Series, https://doi.org/10.1007/978-3-030-77830-9_7

design and management—should be approached from an inter- or trans-disciplinary perspective (DeLue and Elkins 2008; Howard et al. 2013; Antrop, Van Eetvelde 2017). Despite such widespread declarations, academic practice—as well as its extra-academic counterpart—seems to go on with unilateral views offered by individual disciplines that are not likely to reformulate their definitions of landscape in light of other perspectives. This is the case with, among others, the political approach to landscape and the aesthetic one. Even though 'landscape politics' and 'landscape aesthetics' are not mutually exclusive—just as, in general, politics and aesthetics are not (Rancière 2015; Sartwell 2010)—hardly ever do they cross (e.g. Benediktsson 2007, Kühne 2018a, b, Porteous 1996).

The aesthetic approach to landscapes (landscape aesthetics) and the political one (landscape politics) are both well-grounded in contemporary humanities, yet for different reasons. On the one hand, one may still notice an inclination among academics and non-academics to think of landscapes as aesthetic, i.e. as 'objects' that are first and foremost sources of aesthetic satisfaction and hence are defined by their aesthetic (formal) qualities. Such a 'scenic' (Olwig 2019) understanding of landscapes may be seen as the heritage of an art-historical approach and largely results from treating the landscape as an image whose geographical and political senses are coded in its visual qualities and, hence, have to be interpreted 'iconographically' (Daniel and Cosgrove 1988).

On the other hand, such an aesthetic interpretation of landscape is either criticized as misguided or treated only as part of the far more important political aspect of that concept. The political interpretation—in a very broad sense (e.g. Lounela et al. 2019)—of landscape has been dominant in landscape studies in recent decades. A landscape is interpreted mainly as a representation or performance or 'medium' in which political meanings are either created or expressed. A 'substantive' (Olwig 2019) landscape is a 'scene' (not scenery) in which individual or collective political actions take place and which is shaped by them and, as such, is a material and perceptual record of political meanings. This, in turn, means that landscapes have an influence on people who experience them. In other words, every landscape turns out to be political insofar as it bears traces of a polity and is one of its major elements. A political approach to landscapes is thus focused on such issues as who can access landscapes? When and how? Who do they belong to? Who can create and use them and how? Who manages them and how? Who is entitled to interpret them? In this respect, landscape studies follow the agenda of the spatial turn, conceiving of and analyzing landscapes as places or spaces which have a decisive social dimension and function. In other words, in terms of politics, landscapes are seen as matterscapes, mindscapes and powerscapes (Jacobs 2006 in: Voghera 2011), while the last term seems to offer a general frame for the other two.

As mentioned above, political interpretations of landscapes do not usually take into account aesthetic considerations (Bender 1995; Olwig and Mitchell 2016). Even if landscapes' materiality and sensoriality are recognized and acknowledged as important, landscapes are approached in a largely semiotic manner in the sense that what is looked for is the meaning encoded, decoded, recoded in and by them (Cosgrove 1988; Mitchell 2002), no matter whether they are treated as media, representations or performances (Crouch 2013; Waterton 2019). In fact, such an approach leaves little, if any, space for aesthetics, especially if the latter is associated with appreciation of formal aspects of landscapes. One way, however, to include landscape aesthetics in the framework of political interpretations of landscape is—just like in the case of landscape architecture—to think of the aesthetic dimension of landscapes as one of the factors that, on a par with others, make them meaningful in people's eyes. In other words, landscape aesthetics, i.e. how landscapes look and—consequently— how they are or should be designed and managed, is treated as another perspective from which the abovementioned political questions may be asked and answered. Such an approach is offered not only by landscape scholars interested in reasons for and circumstances of people's aesthetic preferences for certain landscapes (e.g. Frank et al. 2013; Keshtkaran et al. 2017), but also by those who are interested in environmental hermeneutics: aesthetic appreciation amounts to a particular interpretation of a landscape, one that takes it to be the object whose aesthetic qualities are of primary importance (Clingerman and Utsler 2014). In such a case, the aesthetic landscape is, so to speak, absorbed by the political landscape, as if this were the only adequate way to think of a landscape as an aesthetic "object" without falling prey to the errors inherent to the aesthetic approach.

There is no doubt that the 'scenic' approach has many shortcomings, which are particularly easy to see from a political perspective, but seeing it as the only way to approach the aesthetic aspects of landscapes and dismissing their importance on those grounds in favor of the idea that landscapes are first and foremost political is too hasty, effectively throwing the baby out with the bathwater.

I would like to contend that the landscape conceived of as an aesthetic phenomenon has a conspicuous political significance or—to put it differently—landscapes are as much aesthetic as they are political, and no priority may be given to either of these two aspects. Contrary to what seems to be the dominant approach in landscape aesthetics, landscape aesthetics should not be treated solely as a theory concerning which landscapes people find aesthetically attractive and why. Such an approach may in fact add rather little to debates on the social and political meanings of landscapes, even if—undoubtedly—people's aesthetic preferences may say a lot about their situation. It seems much more rewarding to understand landscapes not solely as sources of aesthetic pleasure or displeasure, i.e. as 'objects' whose significance is defined by people's aesthetic preferences, but as phenomena that are, so to speak, inherently aesthetic, i.e., according to the original meaning of the term *aesthesis*, inherently sensory. It is from such a perspective that landscapes turn out to be political at their core, since they are shaped by politics and so are the sensory (aesthetic) experiences they offer. Thus, I believe that landscape aesthetics should play a conspicuous role in thinking about landscapes and, therefore, make an important contribution to landscape theory dominated by sociological, economic, cultural etc. approaches. Discovering landscapes to be aesthetic and political requires a different approach to landscape aesthetics, e.g. going beyond the traditional view of what aesthetics is. It is precisely the abovementioned 'old-fashioned' (but still quite popular) view of landscape aesthetics that is responsible for the reluctance with which aesthetic aspects of landscapes are discussed by politically engaged landscape scholars.

Landscape and Aesthetics

It is a common thing to open discussions on landscapes with an etymological analysis of the term 'landscape' which offers insight into the history of the ideas behind it (Franceschi 1992; Assunto 2005; Kühne 2018a, b; Olwig 2019). Two main traditions are usually identified: geopolitical and aesthetic. The former is rooted in the premodern meaning of the term 'landscape'. The English term 'landscape' is cognate with the German *Landschaft* and the Dutch *landskip*. While 'land' refers to a stretch of land, '-scape' ('-shaft', '-skip') refers to creation, constitution and condition. Thus, 'landscape' may be interpreted as meaning an area defined not so much by its physical borders as by the customs and culture typical of it. Understood in this way, landscape connotes a bond between a community and its place on the Earth (Olwig 2019).

The aesthetic tradition of thinking about landscape is usually associated with the genre of landscape painting invented in early modern Europe (Gombrich 1966; Jakob 2004; Küster 2010). Even though views of cities, camps, mountains etc. were included in earlier art, they served solely as backgrounds for the main motives; it was only in the Renaissance that landscapes—mainly natural ones—were discovered as worthy of representation. In fact, the term 'landscape' and its counterparts in other languages appear in that time and are used to denote paintings presenting views or vistas. The 'birth of landscape' (Jacob 2004) understood as an artistic genre as well as a cultural phenomenon is associated with the birth of 'landscape sensibility', involving not only appreciation of one's surroundings but also and more importantly a particular attitude towards the world allowing one to appreciate it, namely a distanced, disengaged, purely theoretical approach (e.g. Assunto 2005; Ritter 1974). It was, however, the 18th century that witnessed a rapid development of landscape painting and landscape aesthetics, backed by the invention of landscape gardening that, taken together, may be seen as necessary elements of a 'landscape culture' (Berque 1995). The key category proposed by the theorists of that epoch was 'the picturesque' (Andrews 1990; Frydryczak 2013). It has been decisive for landscape aesthetics ever since as a concept used either to subscribe to or to criticize. 'The picturesque', in fact, meant 'painting-like' (especially like paintings created by artists acknowledged as masters of *paysages*) and implied judging a view in terms of its resemblance to visual art. Undoubtedly, in recent decades that visual perspective has been constantly undermined by the growing number of studies focused on other senses than sight, and yet it still remains the dominant manner of associating the concept of landscape with the aesthetic (e.g. Roger 1997; Nohl 2001; Gobster et al. 2007; Gobster 2008; Skřivanová and Kalivoda 2010; Nijhuis et al. 2011; Benovsky 2016; Petrova et al. 2015; Tribot et al. 2018). The picturesque was a highly conventional way of appreciating surroundings that were deemed noteworthy only inasmuch as they resembled in some respects highly acclaimed artworks. This implied that in order to be considered a landscape a view had to be outstanding, while the criteria to judge it were to be looked for in art that served as an aesthetic paradigm. In other words, the idea of the picturesque involved looking for 'para-artistic structures' (Gołaszewska 1984) in nature or *artification in visu* (Roger 1997), i.e. looking at one's surroundings as if they were an art work and appreciating them that way. 18th-century aesthetics together with its fascination with nature and the idea of the picturesque conceived of as an attractive aesthetic quality is largely responsible for the fact that the idea of landscape is still very often—especially in everyday circumstances—identified with attractive, even spectacular natural scenery or views, which means that sites that are, so to speak, unnatural and/or are found ugly or just plain are thought to be unworthy of being called 'landscapes', in particular when they are supposed to be protected in one way or another.

In other words, a landscape *par excellence* is a natural place that offers views of outstanding beauty, which is the idea behind, for instance, all scenic routes and points. Contrary to the geopolitical approach to the idea of landscape, which is descriptive, its aesthetic interpretation is largely prescriptive. This also explains why cities are often not considered landscapes (*notabene* the idea of urban landscape—and not of cityscape (!)—has gained in importance only recently, while environmental aesthetics was focused on natural environments for quite a long time).

The above approach, termed a 'landscape model of aesthetic appreciation', has been harshly criticized by, among others, Allen Carlson (2000, 2009) and Arnold Berleant (2000, 2005). Their theories have a common root, namely Ronald Hepburn's highly acclaimed article *Contemporary Aesthetics and the Neglect of Natural Beauty* (1966). Not only did Hepburn underline the fact that it was a philosophical error to neglect natural beauty, since nature is an important source of people's aesthetic experiences, he also showed how philosophy erred in approaching the aesthetic qualities of nature in terms of art. He showed that looking at nature as if it were a painted landscape results in overlooking nature's non-artistic qualities as well as misunderstanding the relationship between people and nature. The Hepburnian inspiration made Carlson focus on the former issue, whereas Berleant—as we shall see later—developed the latter.

Carlson criticizes the 'landscape model of aesthetic appreciation' for referring to criteria that are alien to what is appreciated—an environment is by no means a painted view and hence appreciating the former as if it were the latter is inadequate. Following K. Walton's idea that an aesthetic appreciation of art has to apply 'categories of art', i.e. categories inherent to what is appreciated, Carlson claims that an environment should be appreciated as an environment and not as a picturesque landscape. Approaching an environment in landscape terms results in reducing it to its visual aspect and formal qualities as well as treating it as a 'static' entity. Hence, he believes that the term 'landscape' should be abandoned in favor of 'environment', which is free of art-like connotations. An adequate aesthetic appreciation of an environment requires approaching it in a proper manner, i.e. in a manner that is founded on how it is cognized. Carlson's cognitive approach means that people have to have knowledge of the environment they are to appreciate, since otherwise they will not know what they should take into account in their appreciation. For example, if someone wants to appreciate a human environment (or a cultural landscape, to use the idiom incriminated by Carlson), he or she has to have some knowledge of it of the kind offered by anthropology, history, sociology etc. (Carlson 2009).

It is beyond the scope of this article to discuss who is right—the still quite numerous proponents of the landscape model of appreciation, Carlson's followers or 'syncretists' who try to combine both approaches (Carlson and Berleant 2004). What has to be underlined is that in one way or another the landscape (or environment) is conceived of as an 'object' which is aesthetic insofar as it may be subject to an aesthetic appreciation focused on its 'objective' qualities.

As has already been pointed out, the 'landscape model' of landscape aesthetics is still very often identified with landscape aesthetics in general, so it comes as no surprise that landscape scholars interested in political issues find the aesthetic approach useless (apart from historical studies (Bermingham 1987)). It may look, though, as if the approach suggested by Carlson may be more attractive to them than the 'landscape model'. In both cases, a given landscape (environment) has to be studied, because without knowing something about it one is as if blind, unable to identify either its aesthetic qualities or its political meanings. What is more, Carlson's cognitive approach makes it possible to identify aesthetic qualities as determined by politics as one of the factors determining the 'look' of a landscape. Yet, there is a crucial difference between his position and theirs, and it lies in their aims: he is interested in finding out what an aesthetic appreciation of a landscape consists in, whereas they want to decode its meanings. In order to ensure that an instance of aesthetic appreciation is adequate, Carlson has to uncover the meanings of a landscape, which allows one to think that his model of aesthetic appreciation covers the political dimension of landscapes (environments). Thus, the political landscape gets absorbed by the aesthetic one. Instead, landscape scholars interested in landscape politics do not really focus on aesthetic qualities of landscapes as symptoms of political life—which is how they could apply Carlson's approach—but on others' perceptions of and beliefs about these qualities and, therefore, they study aesthetic appreciation as an expression of people's engagement in landscapes. Accordingly, the aesthetic landscape may be said to be absorbed by the political one.

It seems, then, that a perspective treating landscapes as aesthetic, i.e. approaching them as objects that are appreciated for their aesthetic qualities, and the view that sees landscapes as political cannot meet, or—to put it differently—that there is no way for the aesthetic landscape and the political landscape to overlap.

The Aesthetic Landscape

If landscape aesthetics is identified with landscape appreciation as modelled by the abovementioned approaches, then it is indeed difficult to associate it with landscape politics in any other way than it is implied by landscape studies. Landscape aesthetics approached form a political point of view would be thusly defined by such questions as—who is entitled to aesthetically appreciate landscapes? What ways of appreciating dominate and why? Whose appreciation should be taken into account in landscape planning and management?

Even though the issues hinted at by the above questions are undoubtedly crucial, it is possible to understand the link between aesthetics and politics in a much more fundamental way that makes the above questions sound much more serious, that is, treating the landscape as an 'object' which is inherently political because of its inherent aesthetic character. Seen in this light, the above questions concern not so much just one aspect of people's relationship with their landscapes as people's most basic experience of landscapes. Yet, in order to do interpret these questions in this manner, one has to abandon the idea of reducing landscape aesthetics to aesthetic appreciation.

It has been mentioned that Hepburn's article was one of the inspirations for Berleant's criticism of the traditional concept of landscape. Berleant's position in this respect reflects his general attitude towards traditional aesthetics focused on the concept of disengaged contemplation (2004). He claims that this paradigm is flawed since it does not correspond to what an aesthetic experience in fact is. His contention is that an 'aesthetics of engagement' should be developed. One of the fields where he presents this idea is environmental aesthetics.

Berleant juxtaposes the concept of 'observational' landscape embedded in the contemplative model of aesthetics and the idea of the picturesque and the concept of 'participatory' landscape implied by the engaged aesthetics that he promotes. Whereas the former is an expression of the belief that space is abstract, universal, objective, independent of the subject who is a distanced, disengaged observer, the latter is defined by an approach according to which "the landscape is not generated out of an act of consciousness; it emanates from the perceiving body and is infused by that body with its meanings, force, and feelings" (Berleant 2005: 11). "This leads us to a different conception of experiencing environment aesthetically. In this view, the environment is understood as a field of forces continuous with the organism, a field in which there is a reciprocal action of organism on environment and environment on organism, and in which there is no sharp demarcation between them" (Ibid.). In Berleant's view, largely inspired by J. Dewey's pragmatism and M. Merleau-Ponty's phenomenology, a landscape is inherently aesthetic since it comes into being thanks to an aesthetic experience, that is, an experience of one's being physically, sensorily, emotionally and spiritually immersed in his or her surroundings. Such an understanding of the aesthetic character of landscapes implies a different understanding of the aesthetic appreciation of them—it is not so much related to their formal qualities or cultural meanings as it is to how one feels about being immersed in them. In his analyses of environmental aesthetics, Berleant is mainly focused on what makes a landscape aesthetically attractive and identifies what he calls 'invitational features', i.e. features that enhance people's physical and spiritual well-being. It is worth noting that he treats these features not like 'primary qualities' inherent to the surroundings but like 'secondary qualities', i.e. qualities emerging in direct contact with a sentient subject. As such, he claims, they do not fit the subject-object dualism typical for thinking of landscapes in the 'observational' manner.

Berleant's description of 'invitational features' is to a certain degree similar to Böhme's (2017) account of atmospheres. He defines atmospheres as quasi-objects: on the one hand, they are very much like the objects we encounter in our surroundings;

on the other hand, they are not as objective since in order to appear they require the presence of a subject and its experiences, mainly sensory ones. The quasi-objective character of atmospheres makes it possible to design and manage them, much as we do with landscape architecture. In fact, for Böhme, atmospheres are mainly spatial phenomena and as such permeate landscapes. When people like or dislike a landscape, it is because they like or dislike its atmosphere.

Berleant's and Böhme's approaches are similar in that they both think of landscapes as aesthetic in the first place and they both describe the aesthetic qualities of landscapes in such a way as to overcome the subject–object dichotomy (Krebs 2017; Saito 2019; Wilkoszewska 2006). Even if Berleant admits that it is possible to experience one's environment 'observationally', and hence to think of its aesthetic qualities as objective, he opts for the participatory approach, believing that it better accounts for the relationships between people and their environment as well as for the aesthetic qualities of the latter. Böhme also believes that the aesthetics of atmospheres is useful inasmuch as it discovers an overlooked fundamental aspect of human–environment relations.

Both theories are important not only because they are highly revealing and effectively reorient the debates on aesthetic qualities of landscapes and their significance, but also because by doing so they pave the way to bridging landscape aesthetics and landscape politics in theory as well as in practice.

Since Berleant's as well as Böhme's pivotal idea is to overcome the subject–object dichotomy in landscape aesthetics, their theories may be aligned with non-aesthetic theories that define landscape in such a way as to avoid the above opposition. These approaches, developed mainly by anthropologists, archeologists and human geographers and inspired by, among other things, phenomenology, conceive of landscapes as experiential 'entities' (Ingold 2008; Kühne 2019; Tilley 2004; Wylie 2008). Landscape is, then, discussed not as a 'combined work of man and/or nature' which may become the object of someone's experience, whose qualities and meanings do not depend on whether they are actually experienced by anyone, but rather as an 'object' that does not exist independently of people's experiences. In other words, landscapes are thought to be lived spaces that need to be considered from within, that is, from the point of view of people who in one way or another experience them. In this sense, a landscape comes to be in and through interactions between people and their environment. These interactions are always embodied and hence have a thoroughly sensory character. As a result, a landscape can be reduced neither to the meanings that people attribute to their physical environment, nor to its pure material aspects onto which these meanings may be projected. In other words, landscapes are as material, as they are meaningful. A landscape is, then, "a combination of the physical and the phenomenal" (Berque 2006) or "a *phenomenon* which is neither pure representation, nor pure presence, but a result of an encounter of the world and of a certain point of view" (Collot 2011: 18) or "a mixed phenomenon in which reality and imagination, nature and culture [...] overlap" (Le Dantec 2006: 80). In this sense, the landscape can be divorced neither from its objective ground, that is, the objective qualities of the environment independent of anyone's experience, nor from its subjective grasp in someone's experience.

The above perspective on landscapes perforce covers their political dimension due to the fact that "the same land may carry different landscapes" (Le Dantec 2006: 81), i.e. that the same land may be experienced in various ways, which raises a number of questions concerning the relationships between these landscapes or phenomena, if you will: is it possible to harmonize them? If not, how does one resolve conflicts between them? Is it possible to judge some of them more legitimate than others? And landscape politics consist in finding answers to them.

The difference between Berleant's and Böhme's theories and phenomenological accounts of landscapes lies mainly in that the latter take for granted what these two aestheticians focus on, i.e. the aesthetic or sensory character of landscape. If we, nevertheless, treat all these theories as complementary, the questions from the paragraph above may be interpreted in an aesthetic key, different from the one offered at the beginning of this section: is it possible to harmonize various aesthetic experiences of a landscape? If not, how does one resolve conflicts between them? Is it possible to judge some of them more legitimate than others?

It should be remembered that what is at stake here is not judgments of taste and controversies like those encountered in front of painted sceneries, but people's well-being that depends on how they sensorily experience the landscapes in which they are engaged. If we take the above questions to define the agenda of 'substantive' landscape aesthetics, the latter may be seen as a theory as well as practice related to what Berleant calls 'perceptual commons', i.e. the "grounds of perception [...] necessarily, immediately and universally present and accessible" (Berleant 2012: 186). As Berleant justly states, the claims one may make in relation to them are not so much claims about what one likes or dislikes—as is suggested by 'scenic' landscape aesthetics—but rather as claims "to the viewscape as publicly accessible, to quiet public space, for air and water that are pure and beautiful and not altered or controlled for others' convenience or profit; in short, for environment that promotes life and well-being" (Ibid.).

Aesthetics and the Right to the Landscape

What has hitherto been presented as a passage from one type of landscape aesthetics to another made on academic grounds is mirrored in, among other things, the changed manner in which landscape is defined in documents that have been crucial for landscape policies in recent decades.

Berleant's ideas seem to largely concur with the points made in the Council of Europe (2000) as well as in the UNESCO Florence Declaration on Landscapes (2012). These two documents are noteworthy for at least three reasons. First, the political dimension of landscapes is fully recognized in them. Second, they express a particular understanding of the aesthetic dimension of landscapes. Finally, they strongly associate the former with the latter. However, in order to grasp their novelty, one has to mention two earlier documents, namely the UNESCO documents issued in 1972 and 1992 in which landscape policies—or politics, if you will—were defined for the first time (Salwa 2016).

In the 'Convention Concerning the Protection of World Cultural and Natural Heritage' issued in 1972, the term 'landscape' did not appear; the ideas of cultural and natural sites were presented instead. A cultural site was defined as the 'work of man or the combined work of nature and man, and areas including archaeological sites which [are] of outstanding universal value from the historical, aesthetic, ethnological or anthropological point of view', whereas a natural site was defined as a 'delineated natural area of outstanding universal value from the point of view of science, conservation or natural beauty' (UNESCO 2009). The 'sites' were thus conceived of as objects which are exceptional thanks to, among other things, their aesthetic qualities that can be identified by competent observers.

The 'Operational Guidelines' to the above convention formulated in 1992 result from a similar attitude. However, the idea of site is replaced by the concept of landscape (UNESCO 2009). The guidelines are focused on cultural landscapes seen as material expressions of cultures, and, for that reason, the historical values of landscapes are of primary importance. Yet, the aesthetic values of landscapes are also taken into account, as they may be decisive in terms of the Outstanding Universal Values that a landscape may have. Outstanding Universal Value is in turn described as "cultural and/or natural significance which is so exceptional as to transcend national boundaries and to be of common importance for present and future generations of all humanity" (Ibid.). In other words, according to the approach adopted by UNESCO, landscapes (sites) resemble material 'objects' which are to be protected because of their values, including aesthetic ones. The latter are treated as objective and are identified with exceptional beauty. Understandably, this objectifying tendency results from the goals of UNESCO and its conventions which were aimed at identifying cultural and natural material heritage in order to protect it. It does not, however, change the fact that the perspective assumed in these documents is one of an expert who is impartial, disengaged and is therefore supposed to act on behalf of the whole of humanity, adequately identifying the values of a landscape more or less like a connoisseur judging a landscape painting (Olwig 2007).

The above view was challenged by the European Landscape Convention, the preamble of which states that "(…) the landscape has an important public interest role in the cultural, ecological, environmental and social fields, (…) [it] contributes to the formation of local cultures and that it is a basic component of the European natural and cultural heritage, contributing to human well-being and consolidation of the European identity; (…) the landscape is an important part of the quality of life for people everywhere: in urban areas and in the countryside, in degraded areas as well as in areas of high quality, in areas recognized as being of outstanding beauty as well as everyday areas; (…) the landscape is a key element of individual and social well-being and that its protection, management and planning entail rights and responsibilities for everyone" (Council of Europe 2000).

The ELC has been largely hailed as an important step in thinking about landscapes for a number of reasons (e.g. Voghera 2011; Jørgensen et al. 2016; Olwig 2007). From the point of view of landscape aesthetics, two of them are of particular importance.

First, the fact that the idea of landscape is no longer associated with Outstanding Universal Value, and hence—contrary to the UNESCO documents which identified landscapes with sites recognized as particularly valuable according to a standardized set of criteria—landscapes are identified with human environments the values of which and, consequently, the reasons to protect, plan and manage them properly stem from the fact that they are experienced by people in one way or another. Hence, not only is the idea of landscapes dissociated from beauty, the picturesque, sublime or—generally—from the spectacular, but it also turns out to incorporate everyday environments that cannot be divorced from the people who live in them and vice versa.

Second, seeing landscapes as human environments, i.e. as places experienced by the people immersed in them, implies that the aesthetic values of landscapes should not be identified solely with those appreciated thanks to a disinterested, disengaged approach supposedly characteristic of an 'objective' expert. Beauty or other sacrosanct aesthetic qualities one would be inclined to 'objectively measure' are important, yet they are not the only ones to be considered—the aesthetics of the everyday goes well beyond them (Saito 2007; Di Stefano 2017); if they are to be taken into account, they have to be approached just like any other possible aesthetic categories, not from the perspective of an external 'connoisseur', but from the viewpoint of people engaged in and with the landscape in question.

These two points are reinforced by a novel definition of landscape. It states in a seemingly simple manner that "»landscape« means an area, as perceived by people, whose character is the result of the action and interaction of natural and/or human factors" (Council of Europe 2000). A subjective factor is added to the standard understanding of a landscape as a 'combined work of man and/or nature'. It is noteworthy that human perception is not included as a supplement whose only purpose is to make the definition somewhat more precise but as the *differentia specifica* making a landscape different from any other natural or humanized environment. If we replace the term 'perception' with 'experience' (which is justified if the latter is understood as meaning sensory and conceptual perception; this is, after, all the original meaning of the Greek term *aisthesis*), then we obtain an explicitly phenomenological definition of landscape. In fact, the way the landscape is defined by the ELC makes it impossible to reduce it either to its objective side or to its subjective one—on the one hand, a landscape exists independently of the people who experience it, since it is the 'object' of their experiences; on the other hand, it exists only insofar as it is experienced. The definition accords not only with the preamble, presenting landscapes as environments in which people are engaged as they constantly interact with them, imbuing them with meanings, but also with other paragraphs that underly the significance of landscapes for people's identities. A landscape, then, is not so much an environment contemplated together with its decoded meanings and adequately appreciated aesthetic qualities, but a lived space inseparable from people who live in it and experience it in one way or another.

It is this understanding of the idea of landscape that underlies the focus on the significance of landscapes for people's well-being as well as the belief that landscapes' "protection, management and planning entail rights and responsibilities for everyone." (Council of Europe, 2000). It is this line of thought that was taken up in 2012 by UNESCO and pushed forward in a succinct manner.

The Florence declaration is the first document that explicitly expresses the idea that people have the 'right to the landscape' and that it is a 'human necessity'. The idea of having a right to the landscape is interpreted in various ways (Egoz et al. 2011, Menatti 2017), but it generally amounts to the belief that everyone should have an equal opportunity to secure and enhance their psychological and physical well-being by having equal access to the 'objective' side of landscapes and by having their way of experiencing landscapes (i.e. their 'subjective' side) respected. In this sense, the right to landscape is related to natural resources as well as tangible and intangible heritage. What is more, it is said that "substantial rights to landscape should concern sensory—visual, auditory, olfactory, tactile, taste—and emotional perception which a population has of its environment" (Déjeant-Pons 2011: 55). The right to the landscape may be then interpreted as one's right to experience, sensorily or otherwise, the landscape in accordance with him or herself. If such an accordance results in a positive aesthetic experience, i.e. an experience that one would like to sustain, then the right to landscape implies that everyone has a right to positive aesthetic landscapes. Landscape politics should then consist in ensuring that everyone may exercise their right to the landscape; this is the aim landscape policies should serve. The political landscape would then be, so to speak, a landscape polity containing various positive aesthetic landscapes. Securing the existence of a political landscape thusly understood is the greatest challenge that landscape politics has to face.

Landscape policies are sometimes discussed in ethical terms. The ethics of landscape is associated with the concept of *ethos*, i.e. the character of the place, and is concerned with landscape ecology and sustainability (e.g. Gill 2017, Thompson 1998) or political issues (Oles 2015). An ethical landscape policy is generally defined as one that respects the character of the place, its inherent qualities or meanings. A landscape is, then, treated as an object whose features are either to be protected or properly managed, which makes landscape ethics quite similar to traditional landscape aesthetics.

When, however, the landscape is understood not in such an objectifying manner but phenomenologically, the concept of landscape ethics acquires a different meaning. The respect with which one should approach a place amounts in this case to the respect one ought to show to the people who inhabit it and the ways in which they experience their landscapes (UNESCO 2008). Thus, the concept of a right to the landscape and landscape ethics imply one another: a right to the landscape may be exercised only when landscape ethics is applied, while applying landscape ethics aims at securing that right to the landscape. Given that rights to the landscape may have various roots and justifications, landscape politics—in aesthetics as in other fields—inevitably demands that one considers what are—as Kenneth Olwig (2011) asks—"the right rights to the right landscape?".

It has to be underlined that landscape policies should be introduced not only at the level of macro-politics, but also—and maybe even more importantly—at the level of micro-politics, i.e. of acts and decisions made by everyone on a daily basis. The ELC states, after all, that landscape "protection, management and planning entail rights and responsibilities for everyone". The right to the landscape is a human right and as such it has to be respected by humans collectively and individually.

The forty years that passed between 1972 and 2012 witnessed not only the rapid development of landscape studies, the growing awareness that landscapes deserve protection, but also a profound change in thinking about the aesthetic values of landscapes, a change stemming from, among other things, new approaches to aesthetics that were developed in these decades, which made it possible to revise the idea of the aesthetic. One consequence of this evolution is the possibility of marrying landscape aesthetics with landscape politics by interpreting the concept of landscape in aesthetic as well as political terms.

If we understand landscapes as lived human environments whose aesthetic qualities are indissolubly linked to people's sensory experiences of whatever kind, these qualities are to be understood as common goods to which everyone is entitled. Thus, landscape aesthetics is no longer just an element of politics, one of the factors sometimes taken into account in political decisions and more often than not treated as less significant than others (e.g. visual attractiveness as a reason for putting into practice such-and-such landscape policies), but its object, a field (Berleant's 'perceptual common') whose shape and accessibility is to be decided by the polity (e.g. landscape policies as instruments securing people's access to aesthetic values). As N. Blanc has put it, when commenting on the ELC: a 'right to aesthetics' has replaced 'the right of aesthetics' (Blanc and Jollivet, 2008: 205).

Conclusions

It seems that there is now a consensus that landscapes cannot be reduced to "areas (…), whose character is the result of the action and interaction of natural and/or human factors", nor can they be interpreted solely in terms how they are 'perceived'. They are as material as they are full of meanings, and as such they are the grounds and objects of conflicts; many of the efforts undertaken in landscape studies have been devoted to identifying and describing these clashes. However, relatively little attention has been paid to the aesthetic dimension of landscapes and the conflicts involved in and provoked by it. This oversight is largely due to a particular view of aesthetics that identified it with the study of traditional aesthetic categories conducted from an art-oriented perspective. Equating landscape aesthetics with aesthetic appreciation of landscapes resulted in conceiving of it as a discipline that belongs to a completely different order than anthropology, human geography or sociology, which have nothing or little to do with aesthetic appreciation. As a consequence, these disciplines divorced the idea of landscape from the aesthetic. Yet, landscapes are material and hence they are experienced sensorily. An aesthetic experience is a ground experience thanks to which one is aware of his or her surroundings—without it a landscape cannot come into being as meaningful and hence cannot turn into a 'battlefield' where different perspectives, interests, needs etc. inevitably contend. Thinking of landscapes not in terms of an appreciation of their aesthetic qualities such as beauty (or ugliness) but in terms of the sensory experiences they offer lies at the heart of such theories as those offered by Berleant and Böhme. By going beyond the traditional paradigm of aesthetics, both philosophers present landscape aesthetics in a new light. Their theories show that even if landscapes may be objects of aesthetic appreciation, it is different from the aesthetic appreciation of artworks in that it refers to how one feels about his or her relationship to his or her landscape. What is more, by putting so much stress on the fact that people experience their surroundings sensorily, they show that the 'perception' of landscapes, without which they do not exist, is not disembodied and extra-sensory. Landscapes are neither like pictures nor like texts.

No matter whether a landscape is thought of as a natural resource or cultural heritage, we experience it through our senses (Rodaway 1994). The above statement is trivial, so trivial that its truth is very often neglected; as a result, it is often overlooked that it is the sensory or aesthetic dimension of landscapes that is the ground and object of conflicts that are much more fundamental than those happening in the realm of meanings. If we think of landscape politics as a field where policies aimed at appeasing or mediating conflicts about landscapes may and should be worked out, then one should start with conflicts between various aesthetic experiences. Of course, it would be naïve to believe that such conflicts may be eliminated, nevertheless it is quite reasonable to assume that the ideal which should be borne in mind while trying to resolve these conflicts should be everyone's everyday right to the landscape, a right understood as the human right to have a positive aesthetic experience of one's environment.

In closing, I would like to briefly mention a fairly recent Polish example of a conflict over a landscape in which aesthetic and political issues have been indissolubly intertwined. The case is all the more noteworthy as it has not been recognized, at least not in an explicit manner, that the clash was, among other things, over a landscape and its aesthetic qualities.

Kruszyniany is a small village in a rural area in the east of Poland in the direct vicinity of the border with Belarus. Its population consists of, among others, a Tartar minority. The spatial structure of Kruszyniany goes back to the 17th century, while its most famous structure is a wooden mosque built in the 18th century and recognized as a historical monument. The village is located in a region quite renowned for its landscape qualities, resulting mainly from the fact that its nature has not been spoiled by industry. In fact, the surroundings of the village are qualified as a protected area under "Natura 2000".

This pastoral atmosphere was endangered not long ago by an investor's plans to build a large farm where over 100,000 chickens could be bred. For economic reasons, local authorities tended towards backing this project, while the inhabitants of Kruszyniany made efforts to block it. They claimed that, on the one hand, such an enterprise in all likelihood would severely affect the local ecosystem, while on the other—because, for example, of the accompanying odor—it would deteriorate the conditions of their everyday lives as well as discourage tourism. Apart from the fact that the situation was complicated due to the lack of legal instruments necessary for resolving such conflicts, there were a couple of issues that should be noted. First, the village itself as well as its surroundings were not approached as places worthy of landscape protection by either side of the conflict. As an aside, it may be added that the mosque has been recognized as a national historic monument for its historical value, so—from a legal point of view—it stands in a sharp contrast with the surrounding landscape. No one denies that the surroundings (or to be precise: certain sites) are historically interesting and aesthetically attractive, especially in tourists' eyes, but at the same time they are far from spectacular. It seems then that the only reason why this area may deserve special attention is its ecological value. Second, the question of odor tended to be treated as a down to earth 'technical' matter that may, in fact, be a nuisance, but was not considered a fundamental issue that could affect not only the environment but also the local community. Even if the effect of the construction of the chicken farm on the ecosystem may be said to be debatable, it is beyond any doubt that that it would conflict with the right to the landscape possessed—individually and collectively—by the inhabitants of Kruszyniany. The fact that the risk consisted in the ubiquity of an all-permeating odor is significant—the odor, being inevitable, affects everyone and can hardly be effectively avoided. Fortunately, it was ultimately decided that the farm was not to be built—in this case, the 'right right to the right landscape' has been respected.

Undoubtedly the conflict could be interpreted, and justly so, as a confrontation between divergent meanings ascribed to the landscape around Kruszyniany, and hence the innocent looking landscape could be seen as a battleground where economic profit clashed with everyday comfort, centralized politics with self-determination, global perspective with local identity etc. And yet, not until it is acknowledged that such conflicts as the one above are about landscapes as environments whose aesthetic qualities are as important as other assets and that people have the right to live in landscapes that they recognize as spiritually and physically beneficial for them will these conflicts be reduced to economic, technical and ecological issues. As a result, decisions concerning landscape management, protection and planning, that is, landscape politics, run the risk of missing the mark altogether, as they may impoverish landscapes as well as the people living in them, which contradicts the very idea of landscape politics.

References

Andrews M (1990) The search for the picturesque: landscape aesthetics and tourism in Britain, 1760–1800. Scolar Press, Aldershot
Antrop M (2013) A brief history of landscape research. In: Howard P, Thompson IH, Waterton E (eds) The Routledge companion to landscape studies. Routledge, New York, pp 12–22
Antrop M, Van Eetvelde V (2017) Landscape perspectives. The holistic nature of landscape. Springer, Wiesbaden
Assunto R (2005) Il paesaggio e l'estetica. Novecento, Palermo
Bal M (2002) Travelling concepts in the humanities: a rough guide. University of Toronto Press, Toronto
Bender B (ed.) (1995) Landscape: politics and perspectives. Berg, Providence

Benediktsson K (2007) "Scenophobia", geography and the aesthetic politics of landscape. Geogr Ann: Ser B, Hum Geogr 89(3):203–217
Benovsky J (2016) Aesthetic appreciation of landscapes. J Value Inq 50:325–340
Berleant A (2012) The aesthetic politics of environment. In: Berleant A (ed) Aesthetics beyond the Arts. Ashgate, Farnham, pp 181–193
Berleant A (2000) Living in the Landscape: toward an aesthetics of environment. University Press of Kansas, Lawrence, Kan
Berleant A (2004) Re-thinking aesthetics: Rogue essays on aesthetics and the arts. Ashgate, Aldershot
Berleant A (2005) Aesthetics and environment: variations on a theme. Ashgate, Aldershot
Bermingham A (1987) Landscape and ideology. The english rustic tradition, 1740–1860. Thames and Hudson, London
Berque A (2006) Trajection. In: Berque A (ed) Mouvance II. Editions de la Villette, Paris, pp 101–102
Berque A (1995) Les raisons du paysage. Hazan, Paris
Blanc N, Jollivet M (2008) *Vers une esthétique environmentale*. Éditions Quae, Versaille
Böhme G (2017) The aesthetics of atmospheres. In: Thibaud J-P (ed.). Routledge, New York
Carlson A (2000) Aesthetics and the environment: the appreciation of nature, art, and architecture. Routledge, New York
Carlson A (2009) Nature and Landscape: an Introduction to Environmental Aesthetics. Columbia University Press, New York
Carlson A, Berleant A (2004) The aesthetics of natural environments. Broadview Press, Peterborough, Ontario
Clingerman F, Utsler D (eds) (2014) Interpreting nature: the emerging field of environmental hermeneutics. Oxford University Press, New York, USA
Collot M (2011) La pensée-paysage. Actes Sud., Arles
Cosgrove DE (1988) Social formation and symbolic landscape. The University of Wisconsin Press, Madison
Council of Europe (2000). The European Landscape Convention (Available at: http://www.coe.int/en/web/conventions/full-list/-/conventions/rms/0900001680080621; Accessed: 02 Jan 21)
Crouch D (2013) Landscape, performance and performativity. In: Howard P, Thompson I, Waterton E, Atha M (eds) The Routledge companion to landscape studies. Routledge, New York, pp 119–127
Daniels S, Cosgrove DE (eds) (1988) Iconography and landscape. essays on the symbolic representation, design, and use of past environments. Cambridge University Press, Cambridge
Déjeant-Pons M (2011) The European landscape convention: from concepts to rights. In: Egoz S, Makhzoumi J, Pungetti G (eds) Right to landscape: contesting landscape and human rights. Ashgate, Farnham, pp 51–56
Delue RZ, Elkins J (eds) (2008) Landscape theory. Routledge, New York
Di Stefano E (2017) *Che cos'è l'estetica quotidiana?* Carocci, Roma
Egoz S, Makhzoumi J, Pungetti G (eds) (2011) Right to landscape: contesting landscape and human rights. Ashgate, Farnham
Franceschi C (1992) Du mot paysage et de ses équivalents dans cinque langues européens. In: Collot M (ed.) Les enjeux du paysage. Ousia, Bruxelles
Frank S, Fürst Ch, Koschke L, Witt A, Makeschin F (2013) Assessment of landscape aesthetics—validation of a landscape metrics-based assessment by visual estimation of the scenic beauty. Ecol Indic 32: 222–231
Frydryczak B (2013) *Krajobraz: Od estetyki the picturesque do doświadczenia topograficznego*. Wydawnictwo PTPN, Poznań
Gill K (2017) An ethics of landscape architecture. J Landsc Arch 12(3):4–5
Gobster P (2008) Yellowstone hotspot: reflections on scenic beauty, ecology, and the aesthetic experience of landscape. Landsc J 27:291–308

Gobster P, Nassauer J, Daniel T, Fry G (2007) The shared landscape: what does aesthetics have to do with ecology? Landsc Ecol 22:959–972

Gołaszewska M (1984) Estetyka rzeczywistości. Pax, Warszawa

Gombrich EH (1966) The renaissance theory of art and the rise of landscape. In: Gombrich (EH) Norm and form. Studies in the art of the renaissance. Phaidon, London, pp 107–121

Hepburn R (1966) Contemporary aesthetics and the neglect of natural beauty. In: Williams B, Montefiore A (eds) British analytical philosophy. Routledge and Kegan Paul, London, pp 285–310

Ingold T (2008) The perception of the environment: Essays on livelihood, dwelling and skill. Routledge, London

Jacobs M (2006) The production of mindscapes: a comprehensive theory of landscape experience. Wageningen (doctoral thesis unpublished)

Jakob M (2004) L'émergence du paysage. Infolio Éditions, Gollion

Jørgensen K, Clemetsen M, Thorén KH, Richardson T (2016) Mainstreaming landscape through the European Landscape Convention. Routledge, New York

Keshtkaran R, Habibi A, Sharif H (2017) Aesthetic preferences for visual quality of urban landscape in Derak High-Rise Buildings (Shiraz). J Sustain Dev. 10.94.10.5539/jsd.v10n5p94

Krebs A (2017) Aesthetics and ethics of landscape. In: Dürbeck G, Stobbe U, Zapf H, Zemanek E (eds.) Ecological thought in German literature and culture. Lexington Books, Lanham, pp 111–118

Kühne O (2018a) Landscape theories. a brief introduction. Springer, Wiesbaden

Kühne O (2018b) Landscape and power in geographical space as a social-aesthetic construct. Springer, Cham

Kühne O (2019) Landscape theories: a brief introduction. Springer, Wiesbaden

Küster H (2010) Piccola storia del paesaggio. In: D'Alessandro C (trad.).Donzelli Editore, Roma

Le Dantec J-P (2006) Philosophie du paysage. In: Berque A (ed) Mouvance II. Editions de la Villette, Paris, pp 80–83

Lounela A, In Berglund EK, In Kallinen T (eds) (2019) Dwelling in political landscapes: contemporary anthropological perspectives. Helsinki Finnish Literature Society, Helsinki

Menatti L (2017) Landscape: from common good to human right. Int J Commons 11(2):641–683

Mitchell WJT (ed) (2002) Landscape and power. The University of Chicago Press, Chicago

Mitchell WJT (2009) Landscape and power. Univ. of Chicago Press, Chicago, Ill

Nijhuis S, Van Lammeren R, Van der Hoeven F (2011) Exploring the visual landscape: advances in physiognomic landscape research in the Netherlands. IOS Press, Delft

Nohl W (2001) Sustainable landscape use and aesthetic perception–preliminary reflections on future landscape aesthetics. Landsc Urban Plan 54(1–4):223–237

Oles T (2015) Walls: enclosure and ethics in the modern landscape. University of Chicago Press, Chicago

Olwig KR (2007) The practice of landscape 'conventions' and the just landscape: the case of the european landscape convention. Landsc Res 5 32:579–594

Olwig KR (2011) The right rights to the right landscape? In: Makhzoumi J, Pungetti G, Egoz Sh (eds.) The right to landscape. Contesting landscape and human rights. Ashgate, Burlington, pp 39–50

Olwig KR (2019) Recovering the substantive nature of landscape. In: Olwig KR (ed.) The meanings of landscapes. Essays on place, space, environment and justice. Routledge, New York, pp 18–49

Olwig K, Mitchell D (eds) (2016) Justice, power and the political landscape. Routledge, New York

Petrova E, Mironov Y, Aoki Y, Matsushima H, Ebine S, Furuya K, Petrova A, Takayama N, Ueda H (2015) Comparing the visual perception and aesthetic evaluation of natural landscapes in Russia and Japan: cultural and environmental factors. Prog Earth Planet Sci 2:6. https://doi.org/10.1186/s40645-015-0033-x

Porteous JD (1996) Environmental aesthetics: ideas, politics and planning. Taylor & Francis Ltd, Abingdon

Rancière J (2015) In: Corcoran S (transl.) Dissensus: on politics and aesthetics. Bloomsbury Academic, London

Ritter J (1974) Landschaft. Zur Funktion des Ästhetischen in der modernen Gesellschaft. In: Ritter J, Subjektivität. Suhrkamp, Frankfurt/M., pp 141–163, 172–190
Rodaway P (1994) Sensuous geographies: body, sense and place. Routledge, London
Roger A (1997) Court traité du paysage. Gallimard, Paris
Saito Y (2007) Everyday aesthetics. Oxford University Press, Oxford
Saito Y (2019) Aesthetics of the familiar: everyday life and world-making. Oxford University Press, Oxford
Salwa M (2016) The philosophy of landscape. Contemporary perspectives. In: Kołodziejczyk, P (ed.) Definitions, theory & contemporary perception of landscape. Jagiellonian University, Kraków, pp 37–44
Sartwell C (2010) Political aesthetics. Cornell University Press, Ithaka
Skřivanová Z, Kalivoda O (2010) Perception and assessment of landscape aesthetic values in the Czech Republic—a literature review. J Landsc Stud 3:211–220
Tilley CY (2004) The materiality of stone: explorations in landscape phenomenology 1. Berg, Oxford
Tribot A-S, Deter J, Mouquet N (2018) Integrating the aesthetic value of landscapes and biological diversity. Proc R Soc B285. https://doi.org/10.1098/rspb.2018.0971
UNESCO (2008) Québec Declaration On the Preservation of the Spirit of Place (Available at: https://whc.unesco.org/uploads/activities/documents/activity-646-2.pdf; Accessed: 02 Jan 21)
UNESCO (2009) World heritage cultural landscapes. A handbook for conservation and management (World Heritage Papers 26). Available at: https://whc.unesco.org/en/series/26 (Accessed 02 Jan 21)
UNESCO (2012) Florence declaration on landscapes (Available at: https://whc.unesco.org/en/news/943; Accessed: 02 Jan 21)
Voghera A (2011) Dopo la Convenzione europea del paesaggio: Politiche, piani e valutazione = After the European landscape convention: policies, plans and evaluation. Alinea, Firenze
Waterton E (2019) More than representational landscapes. In: Howard P, Thompson I, Waterton E, Atha M (eds) The Routledge companion to landscape studies. Routledge, New York, pp 91–101
Wilkoszewska K (2006) Does eco-aesthetics exist? Diametros 9:136–142
Wylie J (2008) Landscape. Routledge, London

Mateusz Salwa is an assistant professor at the Faculty of Philosophy at the University in Warsaw (Poland). His main field of interest is environmental aesthetics. His recent publications include*Krajobraz. Fenomen estetyczny (Landscape. An Aesthetic Phenomenon)*, Łódź 2019; ""Landscape, Phenomenology, and Aesthetics." *Popular Inquiry* 1, 2022 „What is an Urban Atmosphere." *Contemporary Aesthetics* 8, 2020 (co-authored with A. Andrzejewski); „The ontology of landscape." *Rivista di Estetica 75, 2020* (co-authored with A. Andrzejewski); „The Everyday Aesthetics of Public Space." *Acta Universitatis Lodziensis. Folia Philosophica. Ethica-Aesthetica-Practica* 33, 2019; „Landscapes as Gardens. Aesthetics of the Environment." In *Philosophy of Landscape. Think, Walk, Act*, eds. A. V. Serrão, M. Reker. Lisbon: Univeristy of Lisbon 2019; „Everyday Green Aesthetics." In *Paths from the Philosophy of Art to Everyday Aesthetics*, eds. O. Kuisma, S. Lehtinen, H. Mäcklin. Helsinki: Finnish Society for Aesthetics 2019; „The Aesthetic and Material Implications of Ecoventions' Ongoing Participatory Demands." *Art. Inquiry* 20, 2018 (co-authored with S. Spaid).

The Beauty of Nature at Risk of Extinction! Could Aesthetics Act as a Means for Saving Natural Beauty?

Margus Vihalem

Abstract The article moves within a larger framework of environmental and ecological aesthetics and asks whether perceiving and focusing on nature's beauty could inspire a more sustainable attitude towards nature. Shifting from environmentally indifferent aesthetics to aesthetics that take account of the catastrophic situation of the natural environment, severe threats posed by climate crisis, ever-increasing urbanisation, mass extinction of species, and other related phenomena in a global perspective, will be the guiding thread of the article. Is this new wave of aesthetics—based on the awareness and respect for natural beauty—aesthetically meaningful? Can we conceive an aesthetics that goes beyond the limits of the cultural tradition centred around the primacy of human values and needs? Does this move presuppose a new politics of aesthetics? Is it possible, by changing our attitude towards nature, to initiate a long-awaited change in the general political perception of the environment? A further objective would imply a general and substantial re-evaluation of the natural environment and beauty related to it, as well as outlining a general theoretical framework for achieving this goal.

Keywords Aesthetics · Environmental aesthetics · Nature · Aesthetic value · Human being · Climate change

Is There a Non-Human Aesthetics of Nature?

The whole realm of nature is increasingly at risk and in danger. Massive overconsumption, wide-spread destruction of pristine forests as they are turned into industrially-managed land for food production, as well as the steady—and thus far irreversible—increase of world population, urbanisation and other similar phenomena of global range, have led us to the point of having to ask once-and-for-all: will nature survive these destructive processes? Will global ecosystems be able to survive the enormous pressure caused by the politico-economic system and

M. Vihalem (✉)
Tallinn, Estonia
e-mail: margus.vihalem@tlu.ee

based on the endless growth of consumption? In an era of history, so dominated by human beings over other species, we are entitled to ask: will nature survive the Anthropocene?

When we translate this question into aesthetic terms, we might ask whether there will be any beauty of nature on earth in the longer perspective, and whether there will be anything left for a future beholder of natural beauty. The not-yet-fully-acknowledged imminence of dramatic climate changes on a global scale [and a massive scientific evidence proves that this is undeniably caused by us] is the last and most threatening of signs that something is radically wrong with our values and attitudes concerning nature. Considering something so valuable logically implies taking measures to defend it in order to save it from annihilation. That we act is urgent. Can nature aesthetics as a discipline, and a way to knowledge and awareness, provide us with the means for achieving a more sustainable future? How could a nature-respecting and nature-inspired (eco-)aesthetics help to bring forward a new attitude towards nature? These are philosophical, aesthetic, political and practical questions that call, not only for an urgent answer, but even more for urgent action.

There has been a lot of talk about what is at stake in the present rise of awareness about ecological issues (see e.g., Drenthen & Keulartz 2014). Ecologically responsible thinking has been blamed by conservative political forces for being eager to thwart progress and force us back to some pre-industrial society, devoid of technical devices that proliferate today. This accusation seems naïve and unfounded since it is strictly impossible and inconceivable to abandon all technical progress. Moreover, a return to the past is doubly impossible in a context in which nature has been radically altered and re-designed by us for human needs and purposes, especially in the so-called developed countries. Indeed, there are numerous policies to recreate natural wetlands artificially to preserve some species from extinction by restoring their natural habitat. Nevertheless, the impact of these policies is usually extremely limited, even when attempts are made to recreate the biologically and aesthetically functional environment.

It can be argued that the concept of nature is, by definition, an anthropomorphic concept, dependent on specific cultural conventions and constructs and dominated by the so-called spectator-centred model. It is understood either as only formally opposed to the category of the human or human culture, or to include the category of the human as something that rises (especially in the tradition of Western rationalism) above the essentially chaotic disorder of the realm of nature. The philosophy of art conceived by Hegel is an eminent example of devaluing the realm of natural beauty. The concept of nature thus implies an inherent ambiguity—when we call nature something that is necessarily related to human beings and their interests and is presented from anthropocentric point of view as the principal Other. This devaluation of nature is also reflected in the binary oppositions that guide the Western tradition such as order/disorder, harmony/disharmony, civilized/wild, and so on.

Glenn Parsons, supporting the position of scientific cognitivism, suggests that we stop relying on art-based categories of nature, emphasizing that we must be ready to see traditionally negative aesthetic values of disorder or disharmony as positive values because nature does not follow the model of positive values established by art-based aesthetics. Moreover, Parsons claims that "if scientific cognitivism is correct, then nature represents a vast aesthetic realm that we have barely begun to explore, and whose guiding principles we have only started to comprehend" (Parsons 2007: 14).

In Modern thought, nature and natural order have often been viewed as inferior to human culture, and similarly, natural beauty considered of lower value compared to artistic beauty. That is, considered to have no governing reason, no autonomy, no agency of its own, nature has not been defined as an autonomous subject in its own rights. In this sense, the devaluation of nature and the neglect of natural beauty could possibly be thought of as a privileged focus of feminist studies (see e.g., Lintott 2010) since this neglect reflects the past circumstances of power relations that need to be deconstructed. Especially in the aftermath of the industrial revolution, keen on turning nature into an instrument and resource, nature has been subjugated to increasing demands of humans. The industrialisation of natural resources goes hand in hand with boosting economic development and material well-being. By its very definition economic development ignores the autonomous value of nature as ecosystem; nor does it have any concern for aesthetic value of nature, except as a resource for products that are meant to satisfy certain needs relevant to the human species. In light of this prioritisation of human needs above—and a tragic indifference toward—the inherent value of nature and biodiversity, it is not only necessary to reconsider the definition and meaning of nature, but also essential to reconsider the definition and meaning of human beings and their relationship to nature. It is the whole set of representations and values regulating our interaction with nature (Afeissa 2010) that should be called into question.

Therefore, the question arises—is our (aesthetic) relationship to nature irrevocably anthropomorphic? Are we able to imagine an aesthetic appreciation of nature independent of the set of aesthetic values established by the cultural tradition? Are we able to conceive an aesthetics of nature that goes beyond human beings and culture? It is precisely from an aesthetic point of view that the following thesis can be drawn: our representations concerning nature have been indirect reflexions of human values and for the most part deficient, short-sighted and distorting. Deconstructing this anthropocentric view, one can argue that ecosystems, landscapes, plants and animals can to some extent be regarded as aesthetically meaningful or inherently equipped with aesthetic values as they can be enjoyed as autonomous systems functioning on their own. On the other hand, Yuriko Saito warns us against what she calls environmental determinism, understanding it as a way of thinking "whereby ecological value of an object automatically determines its aesthetic value" (Saito 2007: 83). She argues that attributing an aesthetic value "without reference to the object's sensuous surface" means to confuse aesthetic and ecological values. On the other side, it can be counter-argued that aesthetic value should not be taken as referring exclusively the object's sensuous surface, but of seeing deeper and taking into account aspects that are not explicitly seen, but rather intuited, combining the sensuous with the information that enables us to understand the forces acting behind the sensuous surface. The aesthetic value of a tree cannot be reduced to its ostensible sensuous attributes only, but also must include its implicit sensuous attributes that are objects of (aesthetic) imagination or (scientific) knowledge about the role that this tree plays in the ecosystem overall (see Carlson 1979: 273). The green colour of its leaves can be appreciated also because they refer explicitly to certain chemical processes.

The way is open to recognise nature not as an abstract collection of separate species and individual animals and plants, but as an autonomous system that deserves to be considered as complex and meaningful organisation of diverse ecosystems. Thus, we may argue that ecosystems should be protected, not solely for the benefit of humans, but also because they are beautiful in their living functioning (and in their own right). The beauty of a tree or a bird does not depend exclusively on the human beholder. Extending the meaning of beauty is inevitable while making the beauty of a tree or a bird depend exclusively on the human agency will lead to the inability to recognize the beauty and (aesthetic) value outside of human cognition.

Clearly, we need to re-formulate the question of aesthetic value of nature differently from the past when aesthetics mostly considered art and artworks. We need to take account of the catastrophic situation in order to find a way out of it. What we need is a fresh outlook on nature's value as a whole and in which aesthetics has influence. Instead of focusing on the aesthetic appreciation of one detail or creature and rejecting another, we need to move towards an appreciation of a larger picture. We must be able to reconsider the aesthetic appreciation of nature, to take nature on its own terms. This implies seeing beyond the horizon of our own needs and limited appreciation that grows out of these needs. It also implies a philosophical argument to apply and strengthen the results of empirical research; an approach that demonstrates the scope of degradation and reasons for it. An alternative approach to nature is needed that takes account of the massive degradation of nature, indicating at the same time an alternative way for recognising the aesthetic value of nature. Aesthetic appreciation of nature, defined as "identical with the aesthetic appreciation not of that which is nature, but of nature as nature and not as art (or artefact)" (Budd 2003: 5), could eventually serve as an instrument to recognise the scope of degradation and to outline solutions to escape this vicious circle.

There seems to be no inherent contradiction in the idea that all serious aesthetic appreciation of nature must be scientifically informed and logically consistent, respecting nature's potential for making sense in itself; both as order and disorder and as harmony and disharmony. It also seems consistent to think that the natural environment does not need a philosophical theory to exist. Nevertheless, changing our attitude and policymaking towards nature and its aesthetic value implies both philosophical and rhetorical argumentation to sound consistent. This implies an ability to look beyond the particular aesthetic attitudes (imaginative, functional, expressive and so forth); to reach the point where these different approaches and attitudes merge into an integral picture that encompasses them all. Only then can nature regain its absolute value beyond the narrowly anthropomorphic and utilitarian point of view.

We need not only an aesthetics capable of sensing the beauty of nature as the guiding force of our actions, but also need to invent an appropriate politics capable of preparing this radical transformation in the sensorium that we inhabit. This implies understanding the need to protect and preserve the whole biosphere as beautiful.

Nature as expression of aesthetic values requires that we embrace nature unconstrained by human needs. Nature, beyond the individual species involved, is a biologico-semiotico-aesthetic totality; a living and active whole that makes sense as a whole and forms the sensuous core of the natural environment.

Natural Beauty and Alienation of Human Culture

The aesthetic appreciation of nature was once (especially in the 18th century) an important topic for aesthetics as discipline. Beyond Kant and his declared sympathy towards natural beauty, one of the most illustrative examples of the mentality of the era can be found in the work of Edmund Burke, the author of the much-acclaimed book of A Philosophical Enquiry into the Sublime and Beautiful. Burke takes natural beauty as an object of serious study, stating that "By Beauty I mean, that quality or those qualities in bodies by which they cause love, or some passion similar to it." (Burke 2004: 128). By conceptualising love as a result of contemplating beautiful creatures (and other phenomena) and a resultant mental satisfaction as something different from the desire to possess them, Burke seeks to make a comparison between natural phenomena and phenomena of human culture. Burke considers examples of beauty and the sublime ranging from natural phenomena (birds and animals) to properly human artefacts (buildings). But his examples of natural beauty are mostly restricted to the domestic plants (roses and apple blossoms) and animals (horses, but also swans), thus exemplifying the overall tendency to approach nature anthropomorphically. His analysis of the appreciation of natural beauty is interesting, though it never achieved any systematic form. Neither was it conceptualised to become an integral theory of the aesthetic appreciation of nature. The representatives of the Romanticist movement were probably the last ones to prioritise the natural over the rational.

Ronald Hepburn, in one of the founding texts of environmental aesthetics, explores the reasons why nature disappeared from the focus of the discipline of aesthetics. And he finds this phenomenon to be a symptom of man's alienation from nature, specific to the era of industrial revolution. He states: "The characteristic image of contemporary man, as we all know, is that of a 'stranger,' encompassed by a nature, which is indifferent, unmeaning and 'absurd'" (Hepburn 2004: 286). By discovering this perverted image of nature as meaningless and even absurd, Hepburn manages to diagnose the main symptom in the context of rapid industrialisation and modernisation—that of losing all authentic contact and ties with nature. Nature ceased to be a natural living environment but was turned into a humanised cultural environment; more than mid-way between pristine nature and an artificially designed environment where elements of nature were used as signs of human domination and superiority. Supported by the rise of sciences that gradually obliterated the mysteries of nature, nature ceased to be the authentic place of the sublime or of absolute value. In the Heideggerian terminology, nature ceased to be the home or dwelling of being because it was handed over to instrumental reason.

Deploring the loss of interest in nature's aesthetic value throughout Modern times, we can identify with Hepburn one of the main reasons of the alienation from nature—the uneasiness when dealing with the aesthetic appreciation and enjoyment of nature. Is it not fundamentally a problem of education—the inability to feel empathy? Education plays a considerable role in sensitising us to certain phenomena. We are taught how and why certain processes take place, but we lack an ethical and aesthetic vision of why nature matters. The failure of our aesthetic education can be recognised when, face-to-face with nature, we fail to become involved with nature properly, in its own terms. Unable to understand nature as a complex and highly vulnerable ecosystem, we do not grasp the role played by different actors and agents in the whole that we experience. Instead, we are led, by lack of proper education, to seek in nature a categorisation that is either art-based or has no closer engagement, which has "no active participation in the appreciative process" (Berleant 2013) in order to experience nature aesthetically. The most obvious form of this impoverished attitude is a downright indifference towards nature's functioning and beauty. The overall consequence of this cognitive flaw is that we remain prisoners of our anthropocentric worldview and do not realise that the overconsumption of natural resources leads to a global ecological catastrophe and to the gradual disappearance of natural beauty.

When appreciating nature aesthetically, we are often attracted by the grandiose and the picturesque. We are struck by the great thunderstorm. We are moved by the height and immensity of mountain peaks, the immensity of the sea, just as we are similarly moved by dramatic and tragic actions in theatre. It is a deeply human trait to be affected by something literally larger than life. Another aspect to consider involves the perspective of everyday aesthetics. A landscape that is left on its own appears to most spectators as messy and unclean (Saito 2007: 170). In this instance, enjoying nature aesthetically might imply being or becoming conscious of nature's inherent vulnerability and messiness, its utmost complexity that a small change can possibly affect or even severely destabilise. This is another direction that shows how much aesthetics—in this context, aesthetics of nature—is dependent on understanding the essential vulnerability of the environment. And this is a necessary direction for the aesthetic education to explore. The aesthetic experience of nature has to be an informed one; has to be partly directed by the concern to preserve and protect, and not consume, the aesthetic object.

Ted Toadvine, in his article bearing the title "Ecological Aesthetics," claims that "nature in the pure sense cannot function as a standard for aesthetic appreciation" (Toadvine 2010: 88). He starts by presenting—following Donald Crawford's triple division—the three meanings that the concept 'nature' usually takes on. The first meaning, nature as a metaphysical entity, and as it was represented in 19th century, included the 'unnatural' realm of human culture as part of nature. The second meaning is, properly speaking, Aristotelian—the internal meaning of nature as opposed to the arti-factual and human but including the human body and its natural functions. It is the third determination of nature that corresponds in the best way to what nature is by itself, outside of all human relations and artefacts. This determination, as Toadvine emphasises, serves for an ideal representation of nature, totally independent of all human intervention.

This representation of nature, as always and already humanised, seems invalid for at least two reasons. First, we can perfectly represent nature as not only functioning on its own, but also in no way determined by the presence of human agency. The fact that human culture expands to the natural environment does not mean that nature cannot function on its own. On the contrary, human intervention often changes the conditions of existence for many species, having led to the extinction of many of them. Second, we can imagine hypothetically a total extinction of human species on earth, as we can imagine the ecosystem of the planet Earth ten million years ago when the humans did not exist. So, we are perfectly well positioned to imagine a global ecosystem existing outside of the human culture and influence. Although this is rather a hypothetical representation and not a real situation. A preliminary conclusion could be that nature can be imagined as an autonomous world of its own. Of course, it remains a human concept, but there is something that corresponds to this concept in the reality, outside of the human mental representations. Therefore, we can take nature as a hypothetical or virtual set of values (including aesthetic values) that possess a meaning of their own, depending on their function inside certain aesthetico-semiotic processes. For example, for many species, mating and reproduction processes seem to imply certain aesthetic values and appreciation of a partner as aesthetically suitable. And some authors, starting with Charles Darwin, claim that aesthetic excess (Høgh-Olesen 2019: 45) is implicitly part of life processes.

It remains to ask whether we need to imagine a human being able to perceive aesthetically, as a subject of representations or values that warrants nature as aesthetic phenomenon not per se, but for a rational beholder. This view can easily be criticised because it reserves the faculty of aesthetic appreciation mainly to the human being as a thinking (and sensing) subject. Aesthetics is certainly an ambiguous realm of experience that has traditionally presupposed that the perceiver or beholder is able to produce intelligible concepts that serve to conceptualise different elements of perception, their composition and value. But it can be argued that appreciation is more an intuitive process than a rational calculation and reflection. Thus, we claim that aesthetic appreciation, based on the sense experience and implying a choice, is not exclusively human capacity. John Dewey, in his "Art as experience," presents himself as one of the most resolute proponents of this view, claiming that sense experience cannot be opposed to the intellect, "for mind is the means by which participation is rendered fruitful through sense; by which meanings and values are extracted, retained, and put to further service in the intercourse of the live creature with his surroundings" (Dewey 2005: 22).

Nature is beautiful or sublime, not only in the human sense of the word or from the human point of view. Neither does aesthetic appreciation make sense only from the human point of view. Most of the life-related processes (gathering food, reproducing, growing, taking a specific form, and so on) seem to include basic elements of aesthetic appreciation outside of the sphere of human appreciation. As such, these processes should be recognized as aesthetic-by-definition. Consequently, we are justified to expand the concept of aesthetic appreciation beyond the realm of human culture.

Natural Beauty Versus Human-Centred Beauty

The present era still favours the materialistic beauty of commodities materialised in the countless objects of human artefacts. In other terms, the idealised and immaterial beauty is, in its turn, demised. But it does not mean that we have come to appreciate the beauty of nature and to defend it against all ambition to turn nature bluntly into a resource and economic profit. We tend to prioritise the pleasure created by products of human origin and the contemporary technocratic culture has subordinated natural beauty to the relentless logic of economy and market. The beauty of nature is subject to economic evaluation and often seems to bear a price tag. Subject to economic calculation, the beauty of nature, (generally referring to the variety of natural beings and phenomena), is subject to an accelerating process of destruction or annihilation.

The question of the politics of aesthetics thus turns into the question of politics and aesthetics of environment. Or to be more precise, into a question of politics of aesthetics of environment. The Western philosophical and cultural tradition has thought of nature as something that is there mostly for the human being, as a mere background that the human must endow with meaning and status. In this manner, nature has been reduced to an epiphenomenon of human being, having no intrinsic value of its own. Aesthetic appreciation in this context serves to point to natural phenomena that somehow appear as meaningful inside the human culture.

The unprecedented expansion of urban landscapes and destruction of natural habitat (forests, wetlands, inland and sea waters due to acidification caused by nitric and carbon-based polluters) seems to be the undisputable common denominator of the present time and will lead to consequences that endanger the whole of global ecosystem. By a paradox inherent to the development on Western aesthetics, politics and theoretical thinking in general, natural beauty or beauty found in the (pristine) nature, has suffered from a long and large-scale under-estimation. The beauty of nature has been subjected to the primacy of economic value of nature. Whereas, in industry-driven modernity beauty has been attributed mostly to human artefacts, natural beauty—the beauty of self-regulating and autonomous nature—has been relegated to a secondary place and suffers an agonising death that we witness in the present-day world, while prone to increasing destabilisation on all levels.

A certain idea of politics has driven this demise of natural beauty and aesthetic values related to nature. According to post-humanist environmentalist thinking, it is partly the humanist concern for the exclusive well-being and happiness of the human being that has led us to this impasse. From humanist concern and predilection for values that essentially reflect the interest of human species in detriment to other species and their right to exist, we have come to overestimate the human species, taking for granted its ability to judge and act in a way that preserves the natural environment.

How to understand the element of beauty when it bears no trace of human action and intervention? In order to define natural beauty, we need to understand how a certain politics of aesthetics (exclusively focused on the human-made artefacts) has been transformed into the politicisation of aesthetics, initiated by Plato who took a definite stance on non-intelligible beauty. In order to understand the underestimation or overlooking of the aesthetic element in the nature, we need to understand the mechanism of politics, as it is the key idea that has shaped our perception of the modern world as mainly the human, anthropomorphic world. We thus come to the idea that the Anthropocene is a result of a certain idea of the politics of aesthetics, based on the assumption that the human culture and its artefacts are more valuable than the plethora of natural beings and phenomena.

Kantian aesthetics plays on this very ambiguity, emphasising the concept of disinterestedness concerning the object that we appreciate aesthetically. Undoubtedly, when we think of nature in terms of disinterestedness, we will be in danger of appreciating nature where no concern for nature's subsistence (or preservation) is included. A different interpretation of Kantian concept of disinterestedness is possible. Namely, can I be indifferent to the usefulness of a beautiful object (nature), but nevertheless appreciate its existence rather than inexistence per se? This is to say that Kantian aesthetics seems to imply that the object of aesthetic experience or appreciation might not exist per se and exists only so far as it affects the aesthetic appreciation. Natural objects like landscapes, trees or animals may or may not exist, but it is only as existing or real objects that they become objects of aesthetic appreciation. I will be able to imagine distant places and objects in these places but my aesthetic appreciation of these objects and places remains abstract. It is the right distance that counts as the basis of aesthetic enjoyment. This is where Benjamin's definition of auratic experience—"als einmalige Erscheinung einer Ferne, so nah sie sein mag" (Benjamin 2002: 357) seems to deploy its deep and proper meaning. That is, aesthetic experience of nature is the most intimate and most engaging when we are at the right distance from it.

The Potential of the Aesthetics of Nature

We now come to the potential of aesthetics—particularly environmental aesthetics—in the fight against policies that have led to the large-scale destruction of environment and to the acceleration of the extinction of species. There is nothing new in the interrelation of the arts and environment. The natural environment has for a long time been one of the topics of predilection for art and aesthetics. Nevertheless, natural environment has not been the main object of the arts, nor has it been conceptualised in the traditional aesthetics as possessing a value on its own. It has rather been a back-ground of human thoughts and actions. Even aesthetic appreciation itself has for a long time overlooked natural environment as an inherent (aesthetic) value. For example, in Western culture, the ideal landscape generally refers to parks and other urban spaces designed by human beings rather than to pristine forests and landscapes untouched by human hand (its counter-tradition running from Romantic movement up to deep ecology movements). The aesthetic has thus been the exclusive reference to the human agency and experience, mostly designating values inherent to the cultural production, and not to the production by nature. By overlooking the inherent aesthetic value of nature, aesthetics has tacitly been an instrument for enhancing and justifying the domination of human over nature and other species. Traditional aesthetics, by prioritising the human and the cultural, has overlooked the natural.

Environmental aesthetics including aesthetics of nature being a recent invention in the framework of aesthetics, marks a realm of aesthetic appreciation and analysis that tends to see human and cultural activities as related to nature and natural environment (by definition). Thus, it also marks a shift in the production and perception of values—the realm of human culture is far from being the only object of aesthetic appreciation, as we need to put the realm of human art and culture back into its original context and re-establish an inherent link between them. John Dewey certainly moves in this direction when drawing our attention to both every-day or ordinary aesthetic experience, but also looking at other species and trying to account for their experience of their surroundings as inherently aesthetic. Moreover, there is a direct link between human beings and animals, this link consisting in a certain basic model of experience. And this model of experience, necessary to fulfil the requirements of a biological organism, are shared by humans and other species alike. This is to indicate that Dewey's thinking provides us with an important intuition that "life goes on in an environment; not merely in it, but because of it" (Dewey 2005: 12). The living being depends on the environment as its condition *sine qua non*. The natural environment thereby becomes meaningful as living environment, as a space of intrinsic, non-human value.

Nature, as the natural environment of a living being, bears on nature as a medium and realm of aesthetic experience, by nature different from what we find in arts and human culture in general. In contrast, Arnold Berleant states that environment is not synonymous with nature (Berleant 2002: 3), as environment can also cover a wide range of phenomena related to our perception of the surrounding environment—be it urban, rural, natural, virtual or something else. Far from being necessarily natural, environment in Berleant's account designates the environment that surrounds us. Thus, environment is by definition natural. Since we cannot subsist without an environment, we 'naturalise' ourselves in the surrounding environments as well as we can in order to survive. For example, we accommodate ourselves to feel at home in urban environment whose aesthetics includes noises, toxic gases, and highly standardised norms regulating the construction of buildings and streets.

An environment that has suffered a minimum intervention or involvement of human agency is certainly rare in the present world. Nevertheless, it is logically possible to imagine a pristine environment that has never been touched by human hand or foot. So what we designate as 'natural environment' or nature here is not just some kind of surroundings around us. We designate by environment the natural environment, as it has escaped the human design and destruction and subsists on his own. Natural environment, as we use the term, is not only an aesthetic concept, but also a political concept as it implies the idea that human involvement is perceived as negative. We thus consider human design as secondary (and often harmful), destroying the creative or transforming autonomy inherent to nature. This is how we define the object of environmental aesthetics; that the object of environments aesthetics is something that is valuable and worthy (in its own right). One could also say that the natural environment does not need human involvement in order to be (potentially) aesthetically valuable. Aesthetic appreciation of nature, focusing on nature as complex environment where every detail may have a role to play, goes beyond the contingency of natural processes. It considers nature as inherently valuable or implying values. Aesthetic value of nature, beyond all anthropomorphic beholders, resides in processes that embrace life. Environment is always a natural habitat of some species. It is not just space of human experience but an affective environment, involving numbers of actors (other species and so on).

The general idea behind the aesthetics of respect towards nature can be found in Baumgarten's idea that "the objective of aesthetics is the perfection of the knowledge of the sensuous as such, this is, of beauty." (Baumgarten 1988: 127). Freeing beauty from all pre-determining principles and opening it up to all that can be sensed, Baumgarten could be interpreted as suggesting the realm of the sensuous as synonymous to the realm of beauty. At least by founding modern aesthetics and giving it a name, he makes a small, but nevertheless significant, step towards recognizing beauty for its own sake. It is through the promotion of the knowledge of the sensuous that we come to understand natural phenomena and beings as related to each other and being part of a larger ecosystem. Freeing ourselves from transcendent aesthetic and moral principles, we come to discover the aesthetic value of nature in its immanence, in the complex relationship of different creatures.

Aesthetic appreciation of nature is multifarious and cannot be resumed within one specific formula. Nevertheless, it can be developed and heightened, raised to the level of superior awareness of nature's inherent dynamics. Starting from contingent instances of aesthetic appreciation of a shiny sea or well-ordered and well-kept parks, we gradually rise to the level of absolute sensuousness, starting to appreciate natural beauty in its own terms and in its most contradictory manifestations and forms, independently from human agency. In contrast to Plato's cognitive model for aesthetic appreciation that started from the manifold and finally achieved the absolute of the intellectual beauty, we claim that the reverse is the case. Starting from the idea of nature as a tangible entity and worthy of exploration, we gradually come to understand nature as existing in its living expressions only. This approach combines rationality and empathy (Couston 2005: 283) as they merge and pave the way to non-individualistic and non-utilitarian attitude towards nature. Nature ceases to be an abstract notion and serves for a reference to all the natural phenomena and beings, as well as their beauty.

Seeing natural beauty as aesthetically valuable and meaningful does not necessarily presuppose seeing (or smelling and so on) this beauty, as it does not necessarily presuppose considering this beauty as being 'contained' in the natural phenomena themselves. If David Hume's substantial critical claim underlying the modern aesthetics that beauty cannot be found in things themselves but must be searched for in the contemplating mind (Hume 1985: 230) is taken literally, it is in vain that we seek beauty in natural phenomena as what we encounter in these phenomena are just some complex chemical processes and transformations that do not encompass any aesthetic values per se. Nevertheless, being able to consider natural phenomena and interaction of living beings universally beautiful, that is, aesthetically valuable without exception, could eventually lead us to respect and enjoy nature as it really is.

It is from an informed and empathetic attitude that a radical change in our relationship to nature will emerge and bring about an eventual improvement of global environmental situation. Aesthetics—and more specifically ecological aesthetics—is not a magic stick that allows us to change the situation instantly. Nevertheless, promoting the aesthetic sensibility based on the ambivalence of vulnerability and creativity (or self-generation through natural selection) will provide us with a sensibility that will project us towards a more sustainable vision of human interaction with natural forces. The crisis is far from concerning humans only, or as the climate activist Greta Thunberg claims, it is time to ask and decide: "What do we want the future living conditions for all species to be like?" (Thunberg 2019: 56). There is no alternative to action. Developing a more respectful attitude towards the beauty of nature in its different forms will contribute remarkably to the change of paradigm and will provide us with a deeper understanding of the aesthetic value of nature that takes account of the natural world as it is, in its inherent richness and beauty.

Conclusion

Aesthetic appreciation—to be considered as one of the basic faculties of human beings—has played a two-fold role in the story of natural disaster we currently face. On the one hand, we have been attracted by the wonders and beauty of nature, which has led us to appreciate nature for its most attractive or overwhelming features. On the other hand, we have not been able to pay enough attention to the fact that this overwhelming beauty is unbelievably vulnerable and is increasingly falling apart due to our ignorance concerning its inherent laws that serve to regulate its course and functioning. Having recognised this deficiency of ours, we might be able to reduce our negative impact on nature exactly because there is an increasing amount of evidence, (including aesthetic evidence) that this destruction happens precisely because we have not been able to appropriately evaluate the vulnerability of the natural beauty. As we are slowly becoming conscious of the ultimate necessity to change our very attitude to nature and reconsider the place of the human being amongst other species, the beauty of nature, taken both as concept and mode of experiencing, will guide us in raising awareness. It suffices to realise that nothing of the human creation can compare to the complex and living beauty of nature—forces always on the move, in constant development and evolutionary change. This is the value in natural beauty at the end of the day—that it is never the same, but endlessly reoccurring in new and amazing forms, of its own accord.

References

Afeissa H-M (2010) De mirabilibus mundi: vers une éthique et une esthétique environnementales. Vertigo 10/1. 10.4000/vertigo.9447
Baumgarten AG (1988) Esthétique. L'Herne, Paris
Benjamin W (2002) Medienästhetische Schriften. Taschenbuch, Frankfurt
Berleant A (2002) Art, environment, and the shape of experience. In: Environment and the arts. Perspectives on art and environment. Ashgate, Aldershot. https://www.academia.edu/12353541/Art_Environment and the Shape of Experience (Accessed the 29th Nov. 2019)
Berleant A (2013) What is aesthetic engagement? Contemporary Aesthetics, 11. https://contempaesthetics.org/newvolume/pages/article.php?articleID=684 (Accessed 30 June 2020)
Budd M (2003) The aesthetic appreciation of nature. Oxford University Press, Oxford
Burke E (2004) A philosophical enquiry into the sublime and beautiful. Penguin, London
Carlson A (1979) Appreciation and the natural environment. J Aesthet Art Critic 3:267–275
Couston F (2005) L'Écologisme est-il un humanisme? L'Harmattan, Paris
Dewey J (2005) Art as experience. Perigee, New York
Drenthen M, Keulartz J (2014) Environmental aesthetics. Crossing divides and breaking ground. Fordham University Press, New York
Hepburn R. (2004) Contemporary aesthetics and the neglect of natural beauty. In Carlson and Berleant, The aesthetics of natural environments. Broadview Press, Peterborough, pp 44-62
Høgh-Olesen H (2019) The aesthetic animal. Oxford University Press, New York
Hume D (1985) Of the standard of taste. in essays moral, political and literary. Liberty Fund, Indianapolis, pp 226–249
Lintott S (2010) Feminist aesthetics and the neglect of natural beauty. Environ Values (Environmental Aesthetics) 19(3):315–333
Parsons G (2007) The aesthetics of nature. Philos Compass 2(3):358–372. https://doi.org/10.1111/j.1747-9991.2007.00073.x
Saito Y (2007) Everyday aesthetics. Oxford University Press, Oxford
Thunberg G (2019) No one is too small to make a difference. Penguin, London
Toadvine T (2010) Ecological Aesthetics. In: Sepp HP, Embree L (eds.) Handbook of phenomenological aesthetics. contributions to phenomenology, vol 59. 10.1007/978-90-481-2471-8_17. https://www.academia.edu/10120385/Ecological Aesthetics 2010_(Accessed 29 Nov 2019)

Margus Vihalem is an Associate Professor of Philosophy of the School of Humanities at Tallinn University. In 2009, he defended his PhD at the University of Vincennes/Saint-Denis in Paris on the transformations of the notion of the subject in the poststructuralist philosophy, supervised by Alain Badiou. His research now focuses mostly on political aesthetics and environmental aesthetics. His most recent publications include *Everyday aesthetics and Jacques Rancière: reconfiguring the common field of aesthetics and politics.* (Journal of Aesthetics & Culture, vol. 10, n.1, 2018) and *Political Aesthetics and Its Applications: the Soviet Collective Farm as a Specific Sensorium* (Methis Studia humaniora Estonica).

The manufacturer's authorised representative in the EU is Springer Nature Customer Service Centre GmbH, Europaplatz 3, 69115 Heidelberg, Germany. If you have any concerns regarding our products, please contact ProductSafety@springernature.com

Printed and bound by CPI Group (UK) Ltd, Croydon, CR0 4YY
25/03/2026
02078174-0017